Erick's Whistle-blowers

Part 4
(2016-2017)

Dr. Erick San Juan, DLitt.
July 2017

Published in July 2017 by
Self-Publisher (POD System) - Tatay Jobo Elizes
Printed in the United States of America under ISBN codes below.
ISBN-13: 978 – 1548544171   +   ISBN-10: 1548544175

Book List - Buy online as paperback or kindle,
Contact: job_elizes@yahoo.com
Websites: http://tinyurl.com/mj76ccq + www.jobelizes.webs.com
+ www.jobelizes6.wix.com/mysite

Notice

Welcome to *Erick's Whistleblowers – Part 4,* a compilation of essays, news, opinions, anecdotes and ideas of **Dr. Erick San Juan**, DLitt, a **DOCTOR OF LETTERS**. He is a prolific writer, a keen watcher of people and events, and full of wits and satirical commentaries. He has vast experience to back up his writings.

I am grateful that he consented that I start publishing his writings taken from his blogs, which he started in 2007 as **ericksanjuan. blogspot.com**. I created *Part 4 of his essays from 2016 to 2017*.

His permission to publish may be withdrawn or cancelled by him as a guaranteed option, and without any objection from Tatay Jobo Elizes, the publisher. All Erick's writings belong to his copyrights and maybe republished elsewhere by him.

Views are expressed by the author alone. Tatay Jobo Elizes does not knowingly publish false information or commit copyright infringement having been given explicit permission to publish this book. Tatay Jobo Elizes may not be held liable for the views of the author exercising his/her right to free expression.

Writings are timeless documents and they act as mirrors of history. I publish and reprint books as they remain relevant anytime. I produce solo-author books, columnists' books, novels, opinions, essays, art books, pictorial albums, family trees, joke books, songhits, biographies, travelogues, reunions, in color or black/white, etc.

Why put writings in a hardcopy or book? And not just in the internet. Well, the hardcopy is there for posterity and availability. Not all use the internet. Sometimes, internet has problems.

I publish or reprint free of charge under POD system (Print-On-Demand). Print is always available and for all eternity, unless the owner or author chooses to halt its publication. Free ebooks are also available upon request and may be given free to digital libraries anywhere. Thanks, TJ, Pub.

About the Author

Dr. Erick San Juan, DLitt.

Email: culdesac0002@yahoo.com.ph
Blogsite: ericksanjuan.blogspot.com

The blog is dedicated to the late *Prof. Renato Constantino* and *Eduardo "EDDIE" Romualdez, Jr.,* FILIPINO PATRIOTS.

DR. ERICK SAN JUAN is a political analyst, book author, writer, forum moderator, TV and radio broadcast commentator. He's the Managing Director of NEWSASIA and a former Director IV of the National Security Council. He's a **DOCTOR OF LETTERS.**

Please listen in to his daily radio program which is aired through DWSS 1494khz AM @ 5:30pm broadcast title, "WHISTLEBLOWER" that broadcasts & tackle current issues, breaking news, commentaries and analyses of various events of political and social significance.

LIVE STREAMING:
http://www.dwss-am1494khz.blogspot.com

Table of Contents

(Descending Datelines, 2017 to 2016)

JUNE 27, 2017

Will We be the Next Syria?

Who could fail to see the parallels between the situation in the Philippines with that of Syria, where the US military, initially prevented from carrying out any sort of military action, eventually got the green light. Thanks to the arrival of a little-known, ultra-violent terrorist group called 'Islamic State' [IS, formerly ISIS/ISIL]. Now the United States believe it has acquired some sort of moral authority for carrying out what amounts to the illicit invasion of yet another sovereign state.

However, that is just the beginning of the strangeness. Many have questioned how IS, bereft of any sort of sophisticated fighting apparatus - not least of all an air force - could have continuously evaded the mighty US military, even as the terrorist convoys traveled across wide-open desert in broad daylight between Iraq and Syria.

Professor Michel Chossudovsky, writing in Global Research, forwarded the question so many people have been asking: "Why has the US Air Force not been able to wipe out the Islamic State, which at the outset was largely equipped with conventional small arms not to mention state of the art Toyota pickup trucks...The Syro-Arabian Desert is open territory. With state of the art jet fighter aircraft (F15, F22 Raptor, F16), it would have been – from a military standpoint – a piece of cake, a rapid and expedient surgical operation, which would have decimated the Islamic State convoys in a matter of hours.

Instead, what we have witnessed is an ongoing drawn out six months of relentless air raids and bombings, and the terrorist enemy is apparently still intact," Chossudovsky concluded.

For anybody who doubts the veracity of that assertion, a declassified US document, obtained by government watchdog Judicial Watch, shows that US policymakers actually encouraged the growth of Islamic extremist groups as a way to "isolate the Syrian regime."

The heavily redacted document notes, among other disturbing revelations, "the possibility of establishing a declared or undeclared Salafist Principality in eastern Syria (Hasakah and Deir ez-Zor), and this is exactly what

Dr. Erick San Juan, D.Litt.   6

the supporting powers to the opposition want, in order to isolate the Syrian regime, which is considered the strategic depth of the Shia expansion (Iraq and Iran)." (Source: Robert Bridge @rt.com)

Sad to say that predicates are laid for the next Syria and a possible 'regime change'? What could have gone wrong when the US Joint Special Operation Task Force Philippines (JSOTF-Phl) is in Mindanao for the longest time and the so-called Coast Watch Center? Are we taken for a ride here? Who benefits if this overstretched war on terrorism, like in Syria (is now going on for six months already) will also happen in our country?

And despite the statement of President Rody Duterte that the US troops should leave the country soon and directing its foreign policy towards better ties with China and Russia, in the midst of the Marawi City siege, the Duterte administration asked help from Uncle Sam. Even though it was through the Department of National Dafense, but still it was the government that made the request for military support from the US.

From the article "'Dirty Duterte' on the ropes as ISIS, US Special Forces crash the Philippines" by Robert Bridge explains – "Clearly, President Rodrigo Duterte – like Syrian President Assad – is facing the ultimate challenge to his presidency. And considering his past pledge to realign Philippine foreign policy away from Washington and towards Moscow and Beijing, the question is an obvious one: Are those US Marines and Special Forces in the Philippines, which, as in Syria, appeared without invitation, there to help the Duterte government, or do they have other ideas in mind, which will only become painfully apparent when it's too late for the Philippines leader? As is the case with Syrian President Assad, time will tell what is in store for President Rodrigo Duterte of the Philippines. My personal hunch is nothing good."

Now it can be told, Duterte is fighting several fronts, both domestic and international. He cursed some of the world leaders, including the pope and called them names. His war on drugs metamorphosed into a semblance of gang war like the Mafia vs Cosa Nostra, the Mexican drug cartel war, the chinese Triad vs other drug cartel, etc.

Its unusual for a perceived leftist and close to the communists, is being destabilized by CPP-NPA from north to south especially in his home base in Davao. He should stop dealing with the National Democratic Front and instead use his leftist cabinet secretaries to negotiate with the CPP's Central Committee based here.

My unsolicited advice to the president is to stop cursing and playing toughie. I hope by this time, he should have realized that everything seem to backfire. Despite the denial of his people, his health is now affected by too much tension and stress. We have to make him realize that a dangerous 'program' is on and if not controlled by strategic experts which he needed most this time, we could all be part of the so called 'collateral damage' in the process.

Lets get our act together and help save our nation from destruction.

ooooo

JUNE 21, 2017
War Between US and China, Soon a Reality

"On the current trajectory," Allison contends, "war between the U.S. and China in the decades ahead is not just possible, but much more likely than currently recognized." The reason, he says, can be traced to the problem described in the fifth century B.C.E. in Thucydides' account of the Peloponnesian War. Sparta, as the established power, felt threatened by the rising might of Athens. In such conditions, Allison writes, "not just extraordinary, unexpected events, but even ordinary flashpoints of foreign affairs, can trigger large-scale conflict."

Graham Allison's book "Destined for War" (Houghton Mifflin Harcourt) is just one of the many writers, pundits, professors and journalists who wrote books and articles all pertaining to the possible US and China war. Even yours truly had written articles some few decades ago that the US-China war is inevitable. And what it takes is an ordinary flashpoint of foreign affairs that will trigger a regional conflict or a global war in the process.

As I always say, history repeats itself or people repeats history as what great wars in the past showed which is very much true today, when an existing superpower like Sparta (US today) threatened by a rising power Athens (China today), the possibility of a war is not farfetched and with the alliances in place by both countries, it could be very bloody and a lot of lives will be wasted.

Another analysis by Gideon Rachman, the Financial Times foreign-affairs commentator, considers China's increasing clout in the broader context of what he calls, in a remarkably ugly phrase, "Easternization," which is also the title of his well-written new survey (just published by Other Press). The gravity of economic and military power, he argues, is moving from West to East. He is thinking of more than the new class of Chinese billionaires; he includes India, a country that might one day surpass even China as an economic powerhouse, and reminds us that Japan has been one of the world's largest economies for some time now. Tiny South Korea ranks fourteenth in the world in purchasing-power parity. And the Asian mega-cities are looking glitzier by the day. Anyone who flies into J.F.K. from any of the metropolitan areas in China, let alone from Singapore or Tokyo, can readily see what Rachman has in mind. There is a great deal going on in Asia. The question is what this will mean, and whether "Easternization" is an illuminating concept for understanding it.

One difficulty is that East and West are slippery categories. The concept of European civilization has at least some measure of coherence. The same can be said for Chinese civilization, extending to Vietnam in the south and Korea in the north. But what unifies "the East"? Korea has almost nothing in common with India, apart from a tenuous connection through ancient Buddhist history. Japan is a staunch U.S. ally and its contemporary culture is, in many respects, closer to the West than to anything particularly Eastern. Previous attempts to create a sense of Pan-Asian solidarity, such as the Japanese imperialist mission in the nineteen-thirties and forties, have been either futile or disastrous.

Since nationalism is now the main ideology propping up the legitimacy of China's regime, no Chinese leader can possibly back down from such challenges as Taiwan's desire for independence or Tibetan resistance to Han Chinese rule or anything else that might make China look weak in the eyes of its citizens. This is why Donald Trump's loose talk about revising the One China policy inflamed a mood that is already dangerously combustible. It's worth bearing in mind that "The China Dream" is actually the title of a best-selling book by Colonel Liu Mingfu, whose arguments for China's supremacy in an Asian renaissance sound remarkably like Japanese propaganda in the nineteen-thirties. Rachman quotes him saying that "when China becomes the world's leading nation, it will put an end to Western notions of racial superiority." The only Western power that might stand in the way of this project of Chinese hegemony is the United States. Since 1945, the United States, with its many bases in Japan, South Korea, and the Philippines, has effectively played the role of regional policeman. Partly out of institutional habit, partly out of amour propre, and partly out of fear of seeing its power slip, the United States has had its own issues with nationalism, even before Trump came blundering onto the scene. Joseph Nye, the scholar and former U.S. government official, once argued that accepting China's dominance over the Western Pacific would be unthinkable, because "such a response to China's rise would destroy America's credibility." In a conversation with Rachman in 2015, another American official put this in saltier terms: "I know the U.S. navy and it's addicted to pre-eminence. If the Chinese try to control the South China Sea, our guys will fucking challenge that. They will sail through those waters."

American swagger will always have its enthusiasts. Gordon G. Chang, the author of a 2001 book titled "The Coming Collapse of China," recently wrote a piece in The National Interest that praised Trump effusively for cutting "the ambitious autocrat down to size" during Xi's visit to Mar-a-Lago. Trump, Chang recounts, arrived late to greet his guest. He announced a missile strike against Syria over the chocolate cake. He made Xi "look like a supplicant." Trump may have revelled in this behavior, but Chang's acclaim is idiotic. Deliberately making the Chinese leader lose face, if that's what happened, can only worsen a fraught situation. American bluster—the reflex of the current U.S. President in the absence of any coherent policy—is a poor response to Chinese edginess. Now that China has developed missiles that can easily sink aircraft carriers, and the United States is responding with tactical plans that would aim to take out such weapons on the Chinese mainland, a minor conflict could result in a major showdown.

Dr. Erick San Juan, D.Litt.

China's own attitude toward the status quo is far from straightforward. China may dream of sweeping its seas clean of the U.S. Navy. But, if the alternative is the military resurgence of Japan, the Chinese would probably opt for maintaining the Pax Americana. At the moment, though, the United States itself appears to be drifting. Trump has accused Japan of playing the U.S. for a sucker. He has even suggested that Japan and South Korea might build their own nuclear bombs. But the ex-generals and corporate executives who run his foreign policy seem to favor sticking to the world we know. Both of these policies are flawed. There is no ideal solution to the late-imperial dilemma. But the surest way to court disaster is to have no coherent plan at all. (Source: Are China and the United States Headed for War? By Ian Buruma)

That is the saddest part when leaders are supposed to lead the way for its citizenry's well-being and the country's development but when the leader has no plan at all and be blinded by sheer power and arrogance, hell will break loose and deaths of innocent lives will go to waste.

The pattern of world war is in the offing. The pretext is already there to see. With so many flashpoints, economic crunch, talking about peace but terrorism proliferate unabated, cyber-attacks which could lead to possible banking and stock market collapse, all signs of chaos are now in the offing. Lets all be vigilant..

Ooooo

JUNE 13, 2017
Threat of War is Real

China has for the first time extracted gas from an ice-like substance under the South China Sea considered key to future global energy supply.

Chinese authorities have described the success as a major breakthrough.

Methane hydrates, also called "flammable ice", hold vast reserves of natural gas.

Many countries including the US and Japan are working on how to tap those reserves, but mining and extracting are extremely difficult.

The element, a kind of natural gas hydrate, was discovered in the area in 2007, but this is the first time the country is able to successfully extract combustible ice from the seabed, in a single, continuous operation on a floating production platform in the Shenhu area of the South China Sea, about 300km southeast of Hong Kong, state-run Xinhua news agency reports."

Methane hydrate global sources are estimated to exceed the combined energy content of all other fossil fuels."

Estimates of the South China Sea's methane hydrate potential now range as high as 150 billion cubic meters of natural gas equivalent, sufficient to satisfy China's entire equivalent oil consumption for 50 years.

The commercial production of methane hydrate would reduce China's dependence on energy imports, which accounts for nearly 60% of its crude oil needs, making it the world's No. 2 importer by volume, after the U.S.

Methane hydrate will also aid China's efforts to shift to natural gas from coal, which accounts for nearly 70% of its primary-energy consumption, which has caused harmful pollution to China's cities. China's discovery of methane hydrates off the coasts of Vietnam and the Philippines is what has prompted China to aggressively pursue the occupation of Philippine and Vietnamese shoals and their conversion to artificial islands in order to safely conduct its exploration and production of methane hydrate. This explains China's placement of an oil rig platform off the coast of Vietnam which triggered international showdowns with Vietnam.

The Recto Bank (Reed Bank) area located only 50 miles west of the Philippine island of Palawan is considered a methane hydrate honey pot. The Philippines estimates that the Sampaguita Field within Recto Bank may also hold large deposits of natural gas equivalents in the form of methane hydrates. (Source: Rodel Rodis, Why China will declare war if PH drills for oil)

Now that the question was answered on the real intention of China in the disputed area in the South China Sea especially on our territories, there is no doubt that what

China's soft power approach now with our President is part and parcel of China's 'looting' of our mineral resources.

The threat of war is real because China has already succeeded in extracting methane hydrates (flammable ice) in the SCS and if we will conduct our own oil exploration and extraction, we will disrupt their flammable ice operation in the process.

With our domestic problems on terrorism and the war on drugs, China easily extended help with these two problems. We all know that President Duterte has somewhat gave up on our claim in the disputed areas in the SCS by saying that there is no point of going to war if we are establishing friendship with China. In effect we are allowing the extraction of this mineral by China without doing anything. And not even a joint project? Where is the so called bilateral talks towards bilateral agreement to peaceful resolution of the territorial dispute? Are we taken for a ride here with our full consent? Just asking?

Pres. Rody Duterte should be very careful with his discreet plan of action because so many international think tanks are watching and studying his 'chess game'. One example is the perception that a China inspired revolutionary government was sabotaged by international terrorist organuzation, ISIS.

According to Solgen Jose Calida, Pres. Duterte knew about the plan of the Maute group to attack Marawi. It jibes with my info of a bigger plan of terrorism which could affect the nation.

Even before Pres. Duterte left for his China trip, I alerted him through Sec. Bong Go, NSA Sec. Jun Esperon and other cabinet secretary friends to make sure that my assessment will reach him. I told all of them to reactivate the 'Situation Room' so PRD can preempt any possible threat and mischief.

This plan had been successful during the time of former Pres. Fidel Ramos because of former NSA Joe Almonte's appreciation of strategic intelligence. Any one who knows me and internet information about me will prove me right. Maybe they thought all the while that I was just scare mongering.

Before Duterte left for Russia, he only secured Davao city by putting additional military contingent there. He even brought his top level officials to Moscow and let Budget Sec. Ben Diokno as his caretaker head.

Dr. Erick San Juan, D.Litt.   **13**

When the Maute siege started, Pres. Duterte knew that the Maute's plan is real and immediately returned to Davao. Despite his statement of giving timetable to finish the Maute's it all failed due to the support of the ISIS to the Maute group.

Good thing that DND Sec. Delfin Lorenzana seeked the assistance of the US forces in fighting the real enemy, the ISIS. Despite the noise of the pro-Beijing left, now is the ripe time that the US can prove them wrong by finishing the ISIS terror group before a spill over can reach Metro Manila which could fully destroy Duterte's administration.

There are so many Filipino experts who can be of help. We have to swallow our pride once and for all and tap them for our nation's sake.

This is a matter of sovereignty, we are in a dire strait and we need an immediate solution to this problem. Many soldiers and people died. We have to remind the president that his nationalism is now being tested. We don't even have to give up our mineral resources to anyone, its for our country's future generations. There are other ways than going to war to assert our rights to our resources, there is still time to find solutions to such predicaments.

As Filipinos, this is the right time to do action and unite. Let us help our President, our nation. God bless our country.

ooooo

JUNE 6, 2017
Rumored ISIS In Ph Now

The recent attack at the Resorts World casino-hotel has created another atmosphere of fear now in the metro and we can't blame the public to speculate on the possibility that the ISIS terror group is now in Metro Manila.

The timing is suspect because the ongoing war on terror against the ISIS-linked Maute group et al in Marawi could somehow created the fear that it will reach Metro Manila. So every time that a so-called attack for whatever reason and nature could be linked to the terror group.

Thanks to the NCRPO headed by PNP Gen. Oscar Albayalde, despite the rumored conspiracy theory including ISIS claiming the Resort World tragedy Albayalde's team closed the case by confirming that the mischief was done by a known gambler named Jesse Carlos.

In the February 2016 article of Joseph Chinyong Liow - ISIS reaches Indonesia: The terrorist group's prospects in Southeast Asia he writes – "On January 14, militants killed four civilians and wounded at least 20 in a terrorist attack in Jakarta, in the first successful operation that the self-proclaimed Islamic State (also known as ISIS) has launched in Southeast Asia. For several months, security officials from several Southeast Asian governments had been warning that ISIS supporters might mount an attack in the region. The signs were ominous: increased chatter on Malay and Indonesian language sites expressing support for ISIS, a steady stream of Southeast Asians departing for conflict zones in Syria and Iraq, and the arrest of ISIS sympathizers in Indonesia, Malaysia, and Singapore. Indonesian counter-terrorism authorities had already received intelligence that militants were planning to mount attacks over the holiday period a couple of weeks earlier, which prompted the arrest of several militants and foiled a potential earlier attack.

The fact that Southeast Asia is not yet on the radar of the core ISIS leadership, however, or that the number of Southeast Asians fighting under the ISIS standard pales in comparison with the number of Europeans or Australians, should not be grounds for complacency. ISIS will always struggle to gain considerable popularity in Southeast Asia. The social, political, economic, and cultural conditions in Indonesia and Malaysia are such that the appeal of the ISIS brand of extremism will always remain limited. Even in Thailand and the Philippines, where Muslim minorities suffer more persecution, the conditions they face are nowhere near those confronted by alienated Muslims in Europe.

Even if extremists do eventually create an ISIS in Southeast Asia, its origins will lie not in Raqqa but in the fringes of Indonesian society, in the climate of extremism that reemerged amid the political activism that followed the fall of Suharto, Indonesia's long-ruling dictator, in 1998. In that sense, the threat remains at heart a local phenomenon, even as it may find some form of transnational expression. So although ISIS' ideology will always receive an airing, it will have to compete with radical and extremist groups of various ideological, political, and operational stripes.

Some analysts have warned that competition among presumptive leaders of ISIS in Indonesia will trigger more violence, and there is every likelihood of that happening. Others worry that ISIS may offer opportunities for existing groups to make common cause. This has not happened yet. The fallout between Jemaah Islamiyah and Indonesian ISIS supporters is well documented. But it would be foolhardy to dismiss the possibility of alliances for tactical, if not doctrinal, reasons. There are indications that the rivalry between ISIS and Jabhat al-Nusra in Syria, which Jemaah Islamiyah supports, has started to taper off. There is also evidence that the Indonesian jihadist ideologue, Aman Abdurrahman, has tried to unite disparate pro-ISIS groups. Counter-terrorism establishments in the region should tune in closely to any chatter among Indonesian groups that points in this direction.

The world is transfixed on the possibility, however unlikely it may be, that a transnational, violent network might someday span Europe, the Middle East, and all the way to Southeast Asia. Such concerns are not new: recall the Comintern during the Cold War, and al Qaeda just a few years ago. But the real danger is not that the black banner of ISIS will be raised the world over but that the appearance of ISIS would trigger dynamics among existing jihadist groups and personal networks within Indonesia, possibly joined by groups from the Philippines and Malaysia, that may well escalate into further violence."

And it did happen... the ISIS in Southeast Asia, and now in the Philippines as what Indonesian defense minister told at the Shangri-La Dialogue, an international security forum last Sunday.

Speaking in Singapore amid a bloody standoff between Philippine troops and militants fighting under the IS flag in Marawi city, Defense Minister Ryamizard Ryacudu called the militants "killing machines" and urged full-scale regional cooperation against them.

"I was advised last night, 1,200 ISIS in the Philippines, around 40 from Indonesia," Ryacudu told the Shangri-La Dialogue, using another name for the IS group.

The threat of heightened terrorism, including the impending return of hundreds of Southeast Asian fighters who fought with IS in Syria and Iraq, has been a hot-button issue at the three-day Singapore summit also attended by US Defense Secretary Jim Mattis.

Hundreds of Islamist gunmen rampaged through Marawi, a largely Muslim city of 200,000 in the south of the mainly Catholic Philippines, on May 23 after government forces attempted to arrest their leader, Isnilon Hapilon.

Up to 50 gunmen are still controlling the city center nearly two weeks after the start of fighting that has killed 177 people including 120 militants.

"How can we tackle these foreign fighters? We have to be comprehensive," said Ryacudu, a retired general. "We have to find... complete ways but we must exercise caution, they are killing machines. Their aim is to kill other people so that's why it's our responsibility that we have common understanding, consensus and common proceedings on how to fight these foreign fighters."

Philippine Defense Undersecretary Ricardo David, speaking at the same forum, said the 1,200 figure for total IS fighters in the Philippines mentioned by Indonesia was new to him.

"I really don't know, my figure is about 250-400, a lot less," he told reporters.

But David said there were 40 foreign IS fighters among those who seized parts of Marawi, eight of whom have been killed by government forces.

Earlier, Philippine officials said the slain foreign fighters were from Malaysia, Indonesia, Yemen, Saudi Arabia and Chechnya.

"Our intelligence estimates that there are about 40 foreigners that fought in the Marawi incident," David said. The Philippine official added that the foreign fighters used "back channels" in the Sulu and Celebes Seas near the borders of the Philippines, Indonesia and Malaysia to enter the southern island of Mindanao and link up with local terror groups.

"That's why they were able to muster the operations in the area of Marawi," David said. (Source: Agence France-Presse)

But for whatever its worth, when the Intel Center, an organization of international security analysts leaked to the press that the Philippines is now the 7th failed state, it alarmed me. What a coincidence that another international security group PROTECT had a security forum at MOA and Rohan Gunaratna, a terror expert lecturer confirmed that the ISIS is now in our country. i immediately alerted the president and his key people to activate immediately his SITUATION ROOM as contingency to avert any terror attack while he's in Cambodia, Hong Kong and China. Good thing that he made DOJ Sec. Vitaliano Aguirre as caretaker head. Aguirre has good contact with the intelligence community that averted any mischief while Pres. Duterte was abroad. The rest is an ongoing pocket wars that could escalate like what's happening in Syria and other parts of the world. What happened in Marawi can now be considered another Aleppo.

We all have to be vigilant and help the Duterte administration to stop this stupidity and put an end to terrorism and violence. If not we could be part of the so called collateral damage

Ooooo

JUNE 1, 2017
Terrorism Blame Game

Once again, our country is in the limelight due to the unfortunate Marawi City siege orchestrated by the local terrorist Maute clan/group and supported by the international terror network of ISIS. And it happened while President Rody Duterte is out of the country – in Russia.

While the region is distracted by the missile launching of North Korea, there is far greater problem happening right here in our home, a symbolic move by ISIS from the Middle East to East Asia. But it has been for a while now that President Duterte has been warning that the ISIS terror group is already in Mindanao and the Armed Forces and the Philippine National Police should be ready for any eventualities.

Was the government caught unaware that such group will attack sooner than they expected? Some believe that timing is suspect and that the country is ripe for a regime change. Why is this so?

Remember that Pres. Duterte is very vocal (and can be read also) through his actions that he is gradually pulling away from the claws of Uncle Sam. He also gained several international critics on his war on drugs that his men in uniform (allegedly) are engaged in extra judicial killings (EJK).

Some pundits believe that there are several financiers that is backing the operation in Marawi siege, both local and international. May be some narco politicians and drug lords and those hurt by the president's harsh words and comments.

In the article by Tony Cartalucci, 'ISIS Touches Down in the Philippines', he writes – "Both the Maute group and Abu Sayaff are extensions of Al Qaeda's global terror network, propped up by state sponsorship from Saudi Arabia and Qatar, and fed recruits via a global network of likewise Saudi and Qatari funded "madrasas." In turn, Saudi Arabia and Qatar's state sponsorship of global terrorism for decades has been actively enabled by material and political support provided by the United States."

This arrangement Carlucci added, provides Washington both a global mercenary force with which to wage proxy war when conventional and direct military force cannot be used, and a pretext for direct US military intervention when proxy warfare fails to achieve Washington's objectives.

This formula has been used in Afghanistan in the 1980s to successfully expel the Soviet Union, in 2011 to overthrow the Libyan government, and is currently being used in Syria where both proxy war and direct US military intervention is being applied.

Maute and Abu Sayaff activity fits into this global pattern perfectly.

The Philippines is one of many Southeast Asian states that has incrementally shifted from traditional alliances and dependency on the United States to regional neighbors including China, as well as Eurasian states including Russia.

"The Philippine president, Rodrigo Duterte, cancelling his meeting with Russia is a microcosm of the very sort of results Maute and Abu Sayaff are tasked with achieving in the Philippines. Attempts by the US to justify the presence of its troops in the Philippines as part of a wider strategy of encircling China with US military installations across Asia would also greatly benefit from the

Islamic State "suddenly spreading" across the island nation."

"Likewise, violence in Malaysia and Thailand are directly linked to this wider US-Saudi alliance, with violence erupting at each and every crucial juncture as the US is incrementally pushed out of the region. Indonesia has likewise suffered violence at the hands of the Islamic State, and even Myanmar is being threatened by Saudi-funded terrorism seeking to leverage and expand the ongoing Rohingya humanitarian crisis."

That reported US-Saudi sponsorship drives this terrorism, not the meager revenue streams of the Islamic State in Syria and Iraq, goes far in explaining why the terrorist organization is capable of such bold attacks in Southeast Asia even as Russia and Iranian backed Syrian troops extinguish it in the Middle East.

"With US President Donald Trump announcing a US-Saudi alliance against terrorism – the US has managed to strategically misdirect public attention away from global terrorism's very epicenter and protect America's premier intermediaries in fueling that terrorism around the world."

The Philippines would be unwise to turn to this "alliance" for help in fighting terrorism both the US and Saudi Arabia are directly and intentionally fueling., said Carlucci.

Instead – for Southeast Asia – joint counter-terrorism efforts together would ensure a coordinated and effective means of confronting this threat on multiple levels.

By exposing the deep military industrial complex role in regional terrorism – each and every act of terrorism and militancy would be linked directly to and subsequently taint the 'plotters' in the hearts and minds of Southeast Asia's population.

This paves the way for a process of exposing and dismantling 'state sponsored' funded fronts – including Saudi-sponsored madrasas and some international funded NGOs – both of which feed into regional extremism and political subversion. As this unfolds, each respective nation would be required to invest in genuine local institutions to fill sociopolitical and economic space previously occupied by these foreign funded fronts.

Until then, Asia should expect the plotters to continue leveraging terrorism against the region. If unchecked, Asia should likewise expect the same progress-arresting instability that has mired the Middle East and North Africa for decades.

When the Intel Center, a global organization of top intelligence and geo strategic experts leaked to the international media that our country is now the 7th FAILED STATE, i know that the globalist program is ON.

This is the best time to give our support to our president because no matter what and he needs more prayers and moral support than ever to get through this crisis.

Who wants to be part of collateral damage. Lets get our act together. God bless our country.

ooooo

MAY 24, 2017
China's Double Talk

We are living in very exciting times of war threats and countries being dragged on the brink of actual shooting war. There is the ever threatening North Korea with its stubborn leader and the bully in the region that is making the neighborhood nervous.

In the midst of 'warm friendly talks', President Rodrigo Duterte said that China's Xi Jinping threatened the country of a war if we insist of oil drilling in our territories in the South China Sea. Below is our leader's version of what transpired between Him and President Xi :

"I said, Mr. Xi Jinping, I will insist that it is ours and we will drill oil," Duterte said in a speech in Davao City.

"Sinabi ko talaga harap-harapan, that is ours and we intend to drill oil there. My view is I can drill the oil. Ang sagot sa akin, 'Well we are friends. We don't want to quarrel with you. We want to maintain warm relationship, but if you force the issue we will go to war.' Ano pa bang sabihin ko?"

The mere fact that this incident came from the President himself, still some people 'clarified' the incident as not true or it is not what it was meant to be.

Speaking in Beijing, Chinese Foreign Ministry spokeswoman Hua Chunying sought to make light of Duterte's comments, noting he and Xi had agreed to "strengthen communication" on important bilateral issues.

"During the meeting, leaders of the two countries exchanged views in depth on future development of China-Philippines relations and relevant issues. Both sides agree to strengthen communication on important issues related to the development of bilateral relations, and to proceed in a healthy, stable and correct path of good neighborly relations and cooperation," Hua said.

"In the future, China is willing to make joint efforts with the Philippines to implement important consensus reached by both heads of state, to properly handle disputes between the two countries through peaceful, friendly and cooperative (methods), to continuously deepen and expand pragmatic cooperation in various fields and to push forward a healthy and stable development of China-Philippines relations," Hua added.

According to some reports, even our very own Ambassador to China denied Beijing's bullying. Philippine Ambassador to China Chito Sta. Romana, who joined the first Bilateral Consultation Mechanism (BCM) between Manila and Beijing last week, said there was no threat from the Chinese side during the talks.

But pundits believe that as our Philippine ambassador to China, Chito should have waited for China's ambassador to speak to clarify the incident. "Parang sya ang mouthpiece of China"

"But by own experience in the bilateral talks, [there were] no threats, no bullying, everything was frank but friendly, candid but productive," he told ANC.

"The whole idea...therefore that China was bullying us and threatening us just doesn't pass," Sta. Romana added.

Although the above-mentioned statements clarified that there was no threat, still we have to be wary in dealing with China because Beijing said time and again that they will not honor the ruling from the Permanent Court of Arbitration and that they will settle any disputes only through bilateral talks.

Again, the politicians and the ordinary Filipinos are divided on how to deal with this development in the Manila-Beijing relations. Actually, if we will going to base on the Filipino culture's view on friendship, it is a big no-no that friends treat each other wrongly like giving threats when they feel that their interest is at stake.

On the other hand, it's not only PRRD but some nationalists have already doubts that the US will come to our rescue if China will attack us.

Some pundits believe that China's war threat is baseless due to the fact that China just launched its Belt and Road Initiative and going to war or just merely a war threat is not in their immediate agenda. Peace for development is their top priority for now.

But war or no war threat, the reality is China with its soft power using the One Belt One Road op is actually building an empire to export its surplus, giving soft loans and in the process creating the debt trap. And for those who cannot pay in cash will pay in kind like some land and rich mineral resources. Translation- possibly making the indebted Philippines a province of China without firing a single shot. Be vigilant!

ooooo

MAY 17, 2017
Who Do We Believe?

Tightening the Belt on a Bumpy Road? Who do we believe?

The recently concluded Belt and Road Forum as initiated by and held in Beijing, China promised a lot to boost economies of countries included in the modern silk road. But many economic and political analysts believe that in the long run it is China that will benefit the most in such a huge endeavor.

Billions of dollars in infrastructure will reportedly be given as soft loans under the guise of soft power op to gain confidence among leaders from Europe to Africa and Asia. The much needed materials for infrastructure are already in excess capacity of construction materials from China. Projects outside China are very much needed for these materials and investing on the Belt and Road initiative will favor China's goods to reach the countries in the silk road.

Although reality check, problems may arise in the modern silk road. Unlike before, everything was smooth sailing so to speak. But now several factors have to be considered like terrorism plus the age-old piracy and of course geopolitical aspect as what is happening in the East and South China Sea.

Some other points have to be considered as what was pointed out by Bloomberg's editorial – "The risk, for China no less than participating countries, is that vaulting ambitions could doom the project's chances of success. What's held back infrastructure development in Asia isn't so much a lack of funding but a dearth of viable projects. Inevitably, as it has within China, politically motivated lending will produce more white elephants, burdening host countries with unsustainable debt burdens."

"Strategists might rationalize these losses as the price for support and stability along China's periphery. But the costs may not be so easy to sustain. Fitch Ratings has already warned of the risk to banks' balance sheets as loans sour. Exporting China's investment-heavy development model will also ease pressure on inefficient state-owned enterprises to reform and slash overcapacity. And with China blocking capital outflows and holding onto reserves in order to bolster the yuan, there's simply less money to waste on bad projects.

Nor is there any reason to think that building more roads and pipelines will in itself achieve China's larger stated goals: to promote economic growth and hence political stability. Pouring money into development projects could just as easily encourage graft in countries along the route, fuel anti-Chinese fervor and encourage sabotage attacks. China's historic preference for dealing with authoritarian governments—and raising few questions about their governance—can breed resentment among ordinary citizens, risking future problems.

China's experience with the Asian Infrastructure Investment Bank, one of the main Belt-and-Road funders, is instructive. The institution's flashy launch in 2014 inspired fears that Chinese leaders were seeking to overturn the global financial order. These fears were misplaced. Run by a cadre of international professionals and adhering to high standards, the AIIB is, according to one estimate, unlikely to lend much more than $2 billion annually for its first five years. That will limit its influence, but also its losses.

China needs to apply the same rigor to Belt-and-Road projects, which should be scrutinized not only for their headline numbers but their long-term viability. Lenders need to be transparent about financing terms and considerate of borrowers' ability to repay. Project officers should consult with local farmers, merchants and NGOs, not just bureaucrats, or worse, corrupt leaders; environmental concerns should be aired and addressed. And along with infrastructure, China should be promoting greater openness in economies along the route."

"Most of all, China needs to treat the Belt and Road with care and a clear-eyed appreciation of risk. That will likely result in fewer, less high-profile projects. But they—and China—will be the stronger for it."

Some pundits also fear the debt trap that developing countries may fall into in order to go with the flow of building huge projects in the process. Like in our case there is so much to loose if we will find out one day that our debt to China is so big that we will be compelled under China's conditions especially in our sovereign territories.

Even DLSU Professor Richard Heydarian warned of getting loans from China. Forbes.com also warned that the projected Philippine debt of $167 billion to help finance ambitious programs under Dutertenomics could baloon to $452 billion in 10 years and could lead to debt bondage to China.

Remember the China's Northrail project during PGMA's watch, it balooned to P1 billion despite the project was scrapped.

When China's political clout and 'soft touch op' will be used as leverage, are we really ready to thread the bumpy silk road when China will tighten the belt for us to pay our debts?

Just asking.

ooooo

MAY 16, 2017
Philippines Will Soon be a Province of China?

The Duterte administration has gone a long way in its nine months in office traveling and has already visited 16 countries and garnered around $34 billion in 'pledges' which are combined aid and investments from China and

Japan alone. These travels had cost us $5.5 million or about PhP270 million according to Finance Secretary Carlos Dominguez III. That is supposedly a small investment with big return value. (Source: PCIJ)

The bulk of the pledged investment loans came from China which is in line with China's President Xi Jinping's One Belt, One Road Initiative that will take place in May 14 and 15 in Beijing. Pres. Rody Duterte will attend the meeting after his visit in Cambodia and Hongkong. What is this initiative all about?

"Previously known as "One Belt, One Road", the initiative is being spearheaded by the Chinese government to improve trade and economic integration across Asia, Europe, and Africa. The strategy uses free-trade agreements and infrastructure projects – including roads, ports and railways – to create a modern Silk Road spanning some 65 countries, which have a combined gross domestic product (GDP) of US$21 trillion. It includes both an economic land "belt" through Eurasia, and a maritime "road" to connect coastal Chinese cities to Africa and the Mediterranean."

Through China's 'initiative' countries from different continents can be linked via massive infrastructure projects like high speed trains by land or sea. But according to former National Security Adviser Roilo Golez, it is not as simple as it may seem for those countries that will join the Belt Road Initiative.

"Methinks PRRD will make the Philippines a part of China's 'Belt and Road' plan, make the Philippines its Southeast terminus. This would make the Philippines potentially a part of China's economic orbit which would generate immense economic benefits to the Philippines but would have serious geopolitical and security implications for the country. The overall effect on the country's well being must be carefully studied by the country's economic, security, defense, political, geopolitical and geostrategic braintrust and not decided by only a limited group."

"Should such membership in China's economic orbit come to pass, it would have deep geopolitical and security implications as well as impact on our Exclusive Economic Zone claims especially our one million square kilometer West Philippine Sea, 90% of which China claims, and even extend China's influence on the development and protection of our huge 13 million hectare Benham Rise."

"Such economic engagement would have serious implications on China's achieving its Strategic Triangle Goal and China's geo-strategic move to break out of the First Island Chain towards the Second Island Chain and consequently control of the Western Pacific. This would prejudice the security and geopolitical position of our treaty ally United States and its allies Japan, South Korea, Australia and New Zealand and of course Taiwan."

"Considering the Belt and Road Plan's impact on the Indo Pacific and global balance of power, especially on the status of the US as the hegemon, I do not expect the US to simply sit out and watch the economic and geopolitical consequences to unfold without talking counteraction." (Golez)

Blinded by the economic gains that one country can get from joining the B&RI, that they overlooked the geopolitical implications in the long run. This is what I have been saying all along as a warning that we are the planned future province of China.

Another analysis taken from the article of Malou Mangahas of PCIJ - "Trojan-horse trap?" These days, the Duterte administration is willing to bet that China can turn around its dismal record of projects in the Philippines. But some Filipino scholars on China say the Philippines should be more cautious when dealing with its giant neighbor.

"These are people, companies that felt that just because they have political connections, they can bribe, they can bring all their hanky-panky in our country," commented U.P. political science assistant professor Jaime Naval. "Huwag naman tayo pagisa sa sarili nating bansa (We shouldn't let ourselves be taken advantage of in our own country)."

China is "also very astute like the West and we have to be as astute as them," said Naval, a China and ASEAN specialist. "They're not giving because they love us, they're giving because they take something back."

He recalled reading a study that asserted that "for every one renminbi that China gives as ODA, it gets back six renminbi." Said Naval: "It's a political tool. It's a given. I accept that. But we should not be naive that China is benevolent, that it hasn't wrung us dry."

"There's a big difference between ODA coming from China and ODA coming from Europe, and U.S., and Japan," Naval continued. He said that while "ODA from these developed countries are normally on health and education and certain advocacies that have something to do with the politics of the land and democracy…when it's an ODA from China, it is extractive. There will be digging for minerals, they will get lumber, they will be harvesting natural resources."

Dr. Renato de Castro, who holds the Charles Lui Chi Keung Professorial Chair in China Studies at De la Salle University, for his part observed, "With Chinese deals,'yung binigay ng mga Greeks, sabi nga…'beware of the Greeks giving gifts, it's a trap.' You become dependent on Chinese aid. You become dependent on Chinese market. That's why we become strategically and politically vulnerable to Chinese agenda."

In de Castro's view, "you don't allow someone whom you have a territorial dispute (with) to dominate… this is very dangerous kasi we still have territorial disputes with China so that will give China a leverage in resolving those disputes. That would favor China (and) solve those disputes on Chinese terms, because China has economic leverage." (With research and reporting by Karol Ilagan, PCIJ, May 2017)

That's what make it too complicated in our case (and with the other claimants in the disputed area in the SCS) because we have something that might be taken away from us because we became 'too friendly' with China. In giving too much attention with our economic gains, we overlooked the shortfalls like giving up our territories.

Wake up guys!

ooooo

MAY 9, 2017
War Bells Are Ringing

Mobilization of military hardwares and preparation being done by soldiers are signs that there is an impending war and in the words of Chinese Foreign Minister Wang Yi – "If war breaks out, the consequences would be unimaginable."

The reason for the ringing of alarm bells of a coming war is that major players are on the war games and the world is nervously waiting on who will hit the button and implement the "first strike policy" or will do a preemptive strike on the stubborn leader of North Korea.

The "extraordinary" mobilization of bomber aircraft was reportedly acknowledged by China's foreign ministry, giving no further details.

The general assumption is that China is taking a defensive position in case the US administration of President Donald Trump follows through on its repeated threats of carrying out pre-emptive strikes on North Korea's nuclear facilities.

Traditionally, an ally of the communist government in Pyongyang, Beijing is widely assumed to be protecting its junior partner by flexing a deterrence force against the US. China has openly urged the US not to take unilateral military action against North Korea over the latter's controversial nuclear program.

Beijing has been calling for a diplomatic solution to the crisis on the Korean Peninsula, a crisis which seems to be intensifying following a dire warning this week from US Vice President Mike Pence that the "sword is ready," which was met with reciprocal threats from North Korea that it would "reduce the US to ashes."

Despite calls for diplomacy from China, it is also clear that Beijing is becoming exasperated with North Korea, known formally as the Democratic People's Republic of Korea. China is perplexed by what it sees as the North Korean regime of Kim Jong-Un forming an "epicenter of instability" on its borders.

Earlier this month, there was even an editorial carried by Chinese state-run media warning that China might be forced to launch its own military strikes on North Korea if it comes down to the "bottom line" of preserving stability and security in the region. (Source: Finian Cunningham, Would China Strike North Korea?)

So is it going to be China against North Korea or China versus the US? Just asking.

And the tension among the key players in this war game was intensified in the exchange of words at the UN Security Council meeting wherein China always wanted to resolve the NoKor issue about nuclear missile production and testing through dialogue between US and NoKor thus stopping the US and South Korea military exercises near the Korean Peninsula in the process to ease the tension further. The use of force is not necessary when they can solve the matter through a dialogue.

As reported by Reuters that US Secretary of State Rex Tillerson was dismayed by Wang Yi's tough words is confirmed by his response – "We will not negotiate our way back to the negotiating table with North Korea, we will not reward their violations of past resolutions, we will not reward their bad behavior with talks."

Wang Yi however received strong support from his Russian ally, with Russian Deputy Foreign Minister Gennady Gatilov reported by Reuters to have addressed the UN Security Council as follows – "Russian Deputy Foreign Minister Gennady Gatilov cautioned on Friday that the use of force would be "completely unacceptable."

"The combative rhetoric coupled with reckless muscle-flexing has led to a situation where the whole world seriously is now wondering whether there's going to be a war or not," he told the council. "One ill thought out or misinterpreted step could lead to the most frightening and lamentable consequences."

Gatilov said North Korea felt threatened by regular joint U.S. and South Korean military exercises and the deployment of a U.S. aircraft carrier group to waters off the Korean peninsula.

Both China and Russia also repeated their opposition to the deployment of a U.S. anti-missile system in South Korea. Gatilov described it as a "destabilizing effort," while Wang said it damaged trust among the parties on the North Korea issue.

These arguments between Tillerson, Wang Yi and Gatilov in the UN Security Council, and the toughly worded commentary in the People's Daily, illustrate the folly of the confrontational course the Trump administration has followed towards North Korea over the last few weeks.

Instead of isolating North Korea from China, and getting China to impose tougher sanctions on North Korea, China – exactly as I predicted – is blaming the US as much as North Korea for creating the crisis, and is not only resisting US demands for further sanctions, but is actually increasing its support for North Korea." (Source: Alexander Mercouris Editor-in-Chief at The Duran newsletter online) The North Korea dilemma for the UN and the rest of the world is still in the process of who will be strong enough to hold its reign so as not to start a stronger provocation that may lead us all to another world war.

Although there was an analysis in the past that the next global war will start in the Korean Peninsula aggravated by alliances of the major world powers, methinks that as long as cooler heads treat the situation with utmost diplomacy and reason, humanity can still enjoy a peaceful world... for the meantime.

But many in the know are worried about the global military industrial complex top secret agenda of the war cycle. I was told that "if the program is on, sometimes you can delay it but nobody can stop it."

God forbid!

ooooo

MAY 9, 2017
Duterte's Art of War

In October of last year President Duterte told the Americans that there will no longer be any joint military exercises with them. The cancellation of several joint military exercises with the US, namely the US-Philippine Amphibious Landing Exercise (Phiblex) and Cooperation Afloat Readiness and Training Exercise (Carat) and stopping the US from using Philippine ports for freedom of navigation operations and refusal to allow the US to develop the strategic Bautista Airbase on the island province of Palawan are just among the factors that China are not comfortable with.

Even the ruling of the Permanent Court of Arbitration in The Hague was not tackled by the present leadership when they went to China. Also the decision that our fishermen can fish in the waters inside our economic zone/territorial waters is in the hands of China's leadership, and several other conditions that are favorable to China. So, Mr. President is this what you call 'independent foreign policy'?

And the most recent one when our top defense officials visited our fellow Filipinos in the Kalayaan island group or Spratly, China was quick in saying that we have to ask for permission first from them or we will face the consequences.

I hope that PRRD's 'One step forward, two steps backward' strategy will prosper.

As what was cited in detail by Prof. Richard Javad Heydarian in his latest article Duterte's 'China honeymoon comes to a close – "Weeks earlier, Beijing was openly vexed when Duterte announced with bravado that he will visit and plant the Philippine flag in the hotly-disputed Thitu Island (Pag-asa to Filipinos), the second largest naturally-formed land feature in the Spratlys. The island, which hosts an airstrip and civilian and military populations, has been under Manila's administration since the 1970s. He also ordered troops to occupy and protect Philippine-claimed land features in the area.

Duterte later cancelled his plan to visit the features, in a convoluted nod towards Beijing's displeasure. "China sent word, 'Please do not do that,' Well, in the meantime, just do not go there. Please?'"

Duterte said in explaining his decision to walk back his decision. "So, because of our friendship with China, and because we value your friendship, I will not go there to raise the Philippine flag. Maybe I'll send my son."

Soon thereafter Duterte gave the go-ahead to defense minister Delfin Lorenzana and armed forces chief of staff Eduardo Año to visit the disputed land feature, which China also considers part of its national territory under its wide-reaching nine-dash map. It was the first time in years that top Filipino defense officials traveled to the features. Lorenzana later described the trip as routine."

"We hope that the Philippine side could cherish the hard-won sound momentum of development [in] bilateral relations [we] are experiencing," said Chinese foreign ministry spokesperson Lu Kang in response to last week's visit by top Filipino defense officials to disputed Spratly island features. "[China is] gravely concerned about and dissatisfied with this, [and] has lodged representations with the Philippine side."

The ministry also cautioned Manila to "faithfully follow the consensus" reached between the two national leaders in October last year.

Sec. Ernesto Abella, Duterte's spokesman, fired back by saying that the trip was "part of efforts to improve the safety, welfare, [and] livelihood of Filipinos residing and living in the municipality of Kalayaan," using the Philippines' preferred word for the Spratlys.

In response to reports that a nearby Chinese military detachment at Subi Reef tried to drive away the plane that carried Filipino defense officials, including Defense Secretary Delfin Lorenzana, the president's office said "The Philippines has long been undertaking customary and routine maritime patrol and overflight in the West Philippine Sea," and that they "are lawful activities under international law."

With the budget of 1.6 billion pesos for the refurbishment and upgrade of Filipino facilities in the Spratlys, is a clear sign that Duterte administration is seriously saying to China that we will never just give up our territories because of 'friendship' and 'economics'.

The president should be wary in dealing with big nations like China, US and Russia. He has to calculate his statements which could be music to the ears of some leaders or noise to few that cannot forget.

ooooo

MAY 9, 2017
The Program is On: It's War

Through the years in all my writings and radio broadcasts I closely monitored China's moves either by soft or hard power, influencing countries like ours due to our alliance with the US. Even before the advent of the internet, I have written the imminent war betwen US – China and if that happens all their allies could be dragged into a global war just like in our case. Like what I always say as a reminder that when the program is on, it can be delayed but it will push through just like this war. Unfortunately, the drums of war is getting louder this time and the fear of many is just one button away from a nuclear war.

This is the reason why I never get tired reminding our government and the past administrations that China's goal of making Luzon their province will soon happen if we allow it. I am with former National Security Adviser Roilo Golez in his detailed article – "The Philippines faces a very serious security challenge in two fronts and how it plays out could critically affect the balance of power in the Asia Pacific Region and beyond" referring to the Scarborough Shoal and Benham Rise.

"Golez said of the Chinese activities: "I do not believe the survey ship conducted harmless scientific research contrary to what the Chinese officially announced. I believe it conducted what it is capable of doing to promote China's interest and prejudice Philippine interest."

A former Navy captain, Golez said China had two objectives:

"(1) Oceanographic survey – to determine the characteristics of the undersea, study the thermocline patterns; data on thermoclines are very important for identifying possible submarine hiding areas, which are of critical importance in future submarine warfare in China's so-called First and Second Island Defense Chains;

"(2) Hydrographic seismic survey – to study what could be under the seabed, to determine through sound reflection and refraction possible oil and gas. Considering the vastness of Benham Rise, the likelihood of such deposits is very strong, many times larger than at Malampaya (westside, in Palawan)."

I believe China is interested in Benham Rise because of two strategic reasons:

Oceanographic data for use in future attack and ballistic submarine deployment.

Data on strategic natural resources like: fish (China's food supply is getting very critical) and energy (oil, gas, methane etc. they need alternate supplies to support their rapid industrialization and help ease their Malacca dilemma wherein around 80% of their oil supply can be interdicted or blockaded in the Malacca Strait or even the Indian Ocean)

China's long range plans for sure include soft targets they can seize using hard power or using soft power and skillful diplomacy and alliance building to secure their geopolitical objectives and strategic food and energy resources.

I submit that Benham Rise is one of them. It's a big, strategic objective.

A master of diplomacy like China would certainly aspire to make the Philippines a part of its orbit in the same manner that it is building alliances in the Indian Ocean, far Africa and South America using their soft power.

Why would the Philippines and Benham Rise be of strategic interest to China?

It's because of the geo-strategic concept of The First Island Chain and The Second Island Chain." In China's goal of securing these two island chains, the Philippines is in the middle and the only way to achieve their goal is to annex our country just like their plan with Taiwan.

Benham Rise as I wrote before could be the next Pearl Harbor as we see the confluence of events and the present leadership must be very wary in dealing with China and not believe China hook, line and sinker.

China lied many times before regarding the status of the contested area in the South China Sea, all for civilian use but now it's a military fortress. And God forbid that they will do that again in Benham Rise. Be very wary Mr. President.

ooooo

APRIL 13, 2017
Major Wars In The Offing

Russia and Iran have said that they will respond to further American military actions following the air strike in Syria last week.

The Trump administration has said that more strikes are possible, but Russia and Iran are both pledging that "we will respond with force" if any more attacks are conducted...

In a joint statement, the command center for the two countries and allied groups said: "What America waged in an aggression on Syria is a crossing of red lines. From now on we will respond with force to any aggressor or any breach of red lines from whoever it is and America knows our ability to respond well." (Source: http://www.prophecynewswatch.com)

We are gradually approaching some exciting times and the world is at the edge wherein a tiny spark could ignite the tinderbox that will start a major global conflict. And the newly elected US President plays the major role that may lead humanity to war or peace.

In the article 'Will The U.S. Be Drawn Into Fighting Two Major Wars Simultaneously?' one in the Syrian crisis and the other with North Korea. Sadly, the campaign promise of President Trump of not engaging in regime change on sovereign states, here we are witnessing a possible regime change scenario that will put the world in danger to the next global war. The usual promise of a politician meant to be broken or only fools don't change their mind?

Is a regime change necessary in solving the North Korean crisis? What is at stake for the rest of the world if ever such scenario will push through?

"NBC News is reporting that President Donald Trump is considering various military options for North Korea, and one of those options includes "killing dictator Kim Jong-Un"...

The National Security Council has presented President Donald Trump with options to respond to North Korea's nuclear program -- including putting American nukes in South Korea or killing dictator Kim Jong-Un, multiple top-ranking intelligence and military officials told NBC News.

After seeing what happened in Syria and hearing these threats openly discussed in the U.S. media, what do you think Kim Jong-Un is thinking at this point?

One member of Congress is warning that "millions can die" if a military strike against North Korea goes badly.

Once U.S. missiles begin flying, North Korea can start firing off their nukes and their vast arsenal of chemical warheads almost instantly.

Could you imagine what would happen if large numbers of deadly nerve gas warheads started exploding in downtown Seoul, downtown Tokyo and at U.S. military bases in Japan?

The carnage would be off the charts, and this is a scenario that we want to avoid at all costs.

Unfortunately, it seems like we are coming closer to a conflict with North Korea with each passing day.

In fact, today we learned that an aircraft carrier strike group headed by the USS Carl Vinson is sailing in the direction of North Korea right now...

Amid rising tensions with North Korea, China's nuclear envoy went to North Korea to assess the situation.

The aircraft carrier and its accompanying ships had been scheduled to leave from Singapore for port visits to Australia on Saturday, but Admiral Harry Harris, head of U.S. Pacific Command, ordered the strike group to head north toward Korean waters instead."

If the above-mentioned scenario will develop into a shooting war what comes after will be far greater devastating for the world's economy. Why is this so?

What was not told was the dumping of US dollar by both Russia and China. Suddenly, at St. Petersberg, in the hometown of Pres. Vladimir Putin it was terrorized by bomb explosion while Putin was there.

Is the Korea threat for real? South Korean security analysts said that South and North Korean governments have been in an open communication including relatives from both camps. So what is the US strike force for?

"So what happens if the U.S. starts fighting two major wars simultaneously, the biggest debt bubble in the history of the planet starts bursting, and the U.S. stock market crashes by 50 percent as some analysts are projecting? US super elites are wary that hidden forces are trying to destabilize America. Will this be the main reason that the real major war is in the offing?

Some Americans still have memories of living through the Great Depression and World War II, but most of us have been living in a bubble of peace and prosperity for so long that we don't think that anything could ever come along and threaten our way of life.

And since the election of Donald Trump, interest in "prepping" has dropped to the lowest level that I have ever seen."

We ain't seen nothing yet that is far greater crisis than major wars happening at the same time. And the first strike policy of the US if implemented will burst that bubble of peace and prosperity. And the rest will surely be part of a bad history.

ooooo

APRIL 4, 2017
Tipping Point of War

In the history of the world, several wars were fought in the Asia-Pacific region and with the continuing provocation after provocation between nations especially in the hottest contested area – the South China Sea, the Philippines could be the next battleground in the theater of war between US and China.

As a writer and observer of events unfolding through the years, we have written this war scenario between the US and China as imminent several years ago as we connect the dots so to speak. Unfortunately we are coming to the realization of that forecast, a program that is on and was only delayed but will materialize sooner than we think. With the new hotspot, the Benam Rise, an underwater landmass 250 kilometers (155 miles) off the east coast of the main island of Luzon, are we seeing another Pearl Harbor in the offing?

We don't want to be an alarmist, we are just observing the confluence of events like some pundits who believe that the recent moves of China is not actually helping its Asian neighbors in the process. Instead the whole neighborhood is nervous that a war might broke out any moment. In this case the long-awaited 'Asian century' may take another century to become a reality due to some circumstances beginning with China's aggressive behavior in its military build up in the region and its secret-secret real economic situation.

According to Gary Shilling (Bloomberg) the following are the issues that will make Asian countries uneasy.

"Globalization is largely completed. There isn't much manufacturing in North America and Europe left to be moved to lower-cost developing economies. At the same time, the West is basically saturated with Asian exports, and those countries are competing fiercely among themselves for limited total export demand. Also, exports are shifting among those countries as low-end production moves from China to places such as Pakistan and Bangladesh, much as they shifted out of Japan in earlier decades. As economies grow, a greater share of spending is on services and less on goods.

The shift from being export-led economies to ones driven by domestic spending, especially by consumers, has been slow. Chinese leaders want this transition, but it is moving at glacial speed. At 37%, Chinese consumer spending as a share of GDP is well below major developed countries such as the US at 68.1%, Japan at 58.6%, and even Russia at 51.9%.

There are government and cultural restraints. Almost all developing Asian economies are tightly controlled by governments. Top-down regimes stoutly resist reform and often persist until they're overthrown by revolutions. The current Mao dynasty in China, as I've dubbed it, seems seriously worried about popular unrest due to the lack of promised economic growth and is reducing what little political liberty was previously allowed. President Xi is now the Big Brother with lots of little brothers insuring proper thoughts and actions, even at the local level.

In Malaysia, Prime Minister Datuk Seri Najib Razak is enmeshed in a multibillion-dollar investment scandal. In the Philippines, crime and drug trafficking are so rampant that President Rodrigo Duterte was elected on a platform of eliminating drug dealers, even by murderous vigilante squads. South Korea's former president Park Geun-hye was thrown out over corruption.

Population problems endure. Despite the need for new workers in Japan as its population falls and ages, women are still discouraged from entering the labor force, and Japan continues to be unwelcoming toward newcomers. There's no such thing as an immigration visa despite the fact that 83% of Japanese hiring managers have difficulty filling jobs, versus a global average of 38% in the last five years.

China also has a looming labor shortage and severe limits to economic growth due to its earlier one-child policy, which resulted in about 400 million Chinese not being born. Low fertility rates are also destined to reduce the populations of Hong Kong, Taiwan, Singapore and South Korea. At the other end of the population spectrum are Asian countries like Indonesia and India, whose population is expected to exceed China's by 2022.

Military threats are growing in Asia, and could severely disrupt stability and retard economic growth if they flare up. China is exercising its military muscles by challenging US military influence in the region by, among other actions, building military islands on reefs in the South China Sea. Japan is abandoning its post-World War pacifism and shifting from defensive to offensive capabilities. The Russians are also making military threats. The region contains five nuclear-armed countries: China, India and its rival Pakistan, Russia, and — most troubling — North Korea, which is testing long-range missiles. China isn't happy about that, but it wants North Korea as a buffer between it and South Korea as well as a deterrent to its old foe, Japan.

There may well be an "Asian century" in the future, but don't hold your breath. It took about a millennium for the West to develop meaningful democracy, the rule of law, large middle classes that support domestic economies and all the institutions that are largely lacking in developing Asian lands." (Shilling)

We are living in these troubling and exciting times, and like what President Duterte said several times in his speeches, he is afraid of a miscalculation that might happen among the many warships in some hotspots in the region that could possibly trigger the next war.

We are now on the verge of tipping point. Our country is now perceived as the epicenter of world war in the offing.

May God forbid.

ooooo

MARCH 28, 2017
Beware of the Twin Arrows

If one country could not do anything with geographical matters because it is by far a work of nature, man-made strategy has to be done in order to find solutions to the problem.

In an article "China's Maritime Choke Points" published at GeoPolitical Futures website, the map showing China's maritime choke points best explain why

China created island where there is no land through reclamation and in the process set up military stations which they denied time and time again that they are not militarizing the area.

Based on the map that one can find at GeoPolitical Futures website – "There are two seas to the east of China – the East China Sea to the north and the South China Sea to the south, with Taiwan positioned in between. Air and naval forces based in Taiwan are, at least in theory, able to prevent movement between the two seas. The Taiwan Strait is fairly narrow and movement by the Chinese to Taiwan's east forces China to pass near the Philippines to the south, and or through the Ryukyu Islands to the north. Passage through the Ryukyu Islands could be blocked by hostile naval forces or by land-based aircraft and missiles.

Therefore, China has a naval problem. It must assume that in war, it will have two different maritime theaters of operation, the East and South China seas, and will have difficulty moving forces from one to the other. Consequently, it needs a strong navy."

That is why Taiwan and Luzon (the northern part of the Philippines) are the target future provinces of China in order to achieve its goal of creating a safe passage in the region, translation – Chinese-controlled areas.

"Therefore, it is clear why the Chinese care so much about the Spratly and Paracel islands in the South China Sea. Until they can guarantee that these islands are not controlled by hostile forces, their ability to create a Chinese-controlled channel through the islands framing the South China Sea is limited. They need to clear the islands, both to allow themselves access and to deny anyone the ability to use the islands to cripple operations in the first place. The Chinese are trying to take the first step in guaranteeing their access to the global sea lanes.

China's naval forces remain inadequate for conflict with the United States. The Chinese have adopted an interim strategy of using air- and land-based anti-ship missile systems to keep the U.S. Navy far to the east and south of the choke points. But these missiles are vulnerable to U.S. air and missile suppression. Therefore, the Chinese are combining them with naval operations intended to intimidate regional nations from working with the United States. As we see in the Philippines, these operations have had the opposite effect. But from the Chinese point of view, this does not change the geographic reality and therefore cannot be seen as a failure, but merely reinforcing the core strategic reality.

One alternative option for the Chinese, if they are unable to mount amphibious operations, is to return to a strategy from the 1960s and use support for insurgencies in Indonesia, Malaysia and the Philippines to create political shifts that would eliminate major threats to Chinese movements. But such insurgencies could force an increase in U.S. naval presence in the region." (Ibid)

Could it be that China has something to do with the latest communist insurgencies and bold activities in the country despite NDF? Just asking.

Methinks that the Chinese initiative in the One Belt, One Road operation especially in the new 21st century Maritime Silk Road has something to do with China's plan of creating access to several sea lanes for geopolitical and economic reasons. It has to be done especially if the mighty US is always on the guard to every move of China's military – may it be in sea, land or air.

In the long run Chinese projects that involve several countries in order to help them economically will benefit China more and make the Xi's China Dream a reality. Although reality checks otherwise, China's big problem is geography and it is in this area that will stop China from expanding its reach and bypassing the rights of other sovereign nations like the Philippines.

China's Xi Jinping has been spending a lot for their global propaganda machine like the every Tuesday's whole page ad at Philippine Star and Manila Bulletin plus their weekly China Daily Asean edition being given free in strategic places including 5 Star hotels showing too rosy pictures of China.

But what was not told is the internal problem in China, both political and economic where capital flight continue due to Xi's expansion program of its military industrial complex allies. A big bubble is in the offing.

We have to be wary at all times in order to avoid a scenario that will make us the next battleground of an impending proxy war. We have to support our president at all cost if it will save our country from dangers.

Beware not only about 'Operation Reverse Arrow' of getting the Philippines without firing a single shot through 'soft touch' op and using their sleepers, dupes and rags to riches ethnic pro China families. And worst the 'Operation Twin Arrows' of attacking Taiwan using their own 'Lily Pad' of islands. I don't want to be an alarmist but be VERY VIGILANT!

Ooooo

MARCH 22, 2017
Benham Rise Ruckus

There is so much fuss on the Benham Rise issue that has actually created tensions even President Rodrigo Duterte himself has already said that there is an agreement between Beijing and Manila before his defense secretary, Delfin Lorenzana came out with a statement that the Chinese ship was doing a survey in the area, translation – an incursion.

President Duterte said that the Chinese have no incursion because we have an agreement and that some people are just blowing it up. It was a research ship. We were advised of it way ahead. Unsolicited advice, Who are the "we" here Mr. President? Many netizens are asking. Because the people in your loop, in your cabinet seems at a lost on whatever that agreement was. We mentioned in our past article that foreign policy of the land should involve its people. The perception seems that the "independent" foreign policy that the President wants is also independent from the people – his constituents. And now the President's detractors especially in the social media are attacking him due to this 'decision'.

Even some solons were demanding the Palace on the content of the so called 'agreement' with China to do 'research' in Benham Rise.

Benham Rise is an underwater landmass 250 kilometres (155 miles) off the east coast of the main island of Luzon. In 2012, the United Nations Commission on the Limits of the Continental Shelf approved the Philippines' undisputed territorial claim to Benham Rise.

Some pundits fear that like what happened in the South China Sea, the disputed areas before are now claimed by China and structures were already in place. And it's not farfetched that because of the strategic location of the Benham Rise, China will use it as its listening post, possibly a place for its submarine and believed to be another entry point in grabbing Taiwan (Xi's China dream) in the process.

Pundits believe that PRRD allows such 'incursion' for economic reason because China is good in using 'soft power' to lure other leaders to kowtow to its whims. And unfortunately, our president is perceived being duped due to the billions of dollars loan given by China to help us improve our economy.

We want to help this administration that is why we all have to be vigilant and help our country against people who are taking advantage of our weakness as a nation, particularly our military.

We already given up some territories in the SCS and now this. Could it be that the alleged plan of China's Xi to make our country as its province is true together with Taiwan?

The recent news about what Taipei's defense minister said recently that "China is aiming advanced medium-range ballistic missiles at Taiwan as part of a growing military threat towards the island is very alarming.

The announcement came after Taiwan said for the first time last week that it is capable of launching missiles at China as it warned of an increased invasion risk.

China still sees Taiwan as part of its territory to be brought back into its fold, by force if necessary, even though the island has been self-governing since the two sides split after a civil war in 1949.

Ties have worsened since Beijing-sceptic President Tsai Ing-wen took power last year, ending an eight-year rapprochement.

The DF-16 (Dongfeng 16) is capable of precise strikes against Taiwan and has been deployed by the Rocket Force of the People's Liberation Army, defense minister Feng Shih-kuan said.

Feng told lawmakers the development comes as China "strengthens its weaponry modernization and military hard power". He did not say how many missiles had been deployed or where.

Taiwan has said China is targeting the island with around 1,500 missiles — this is the first time the defense ministry identified the DF-16 as among them.

Beijing has severed all official communications with Taipei since Tsai became leader in May and has been accused of blocking the island's political representatives from attending international events. (Source: AFP 3-20 2017)

We knew about this plan of China's annexation of Luzon with Taiwan for so long and talked about it on our radio program and in writing. The possibilities are getting stronger as we witness the slow but sure way of encirclement of our territories by China using soft 'touch' operation.

Our nation's patriots are urging PRRD not to let it happen under his term not in the future. God bless the Philippines.

ooooo

MARCH 15, 2017
Global War Design

Another global hotspot is brewing and if not manage with cool heads and by strategic thinkers, another regional conflict is in the offing. We are referring to the Korean Peninsula – the North and South Korea that lately has become another tinderbox that is waiting for a 'spark' that could trigger its explosion.

Like the most talked about controversial ADIZ courtesy of China in the region, there is another far worse controversy that is not welcome in the region – THAAD.

In his article "The Korean Crisis and the THAAD Missile Deployment: A Growing Tinderbox in the South", Caleb Maupin writes: "As the first military hardware associated with the Terminal High Altitude Area Defense, commonly called THAAD, arrives in the southern region of the Korean Peninsula, the tensions around and within the region seem to be escalating. A number of ongoing crises in South Korea are starting to take their toll, and could have regional and global implications.

The most prominent source of tension is the new missile system being erected in cooperation with the United States. The narrative in US media surrounding THAAD is that the Democratic People's Republic of Korea, smeared as "the crazy North Koreans," is threatening to destroy the Republic of Korea located in the south. The new missile system is said to simply be a mechanism for protecting a vulnerable, democratic US ally, that faces being wiped out. Mark Toner of the US State Department described the erection of THAAD as "frankly a response to a threat."

Who is mad about THAAD? And Why?

Objections to THAAD are not only coming from Pyongyang. Moscow and Beijing have both spoken up against the new missile system for reasons that are routinely ignored in US media discourse.

South Korea is hardly unprotected and alone. This is the reason why wealthy Koreans are migrating worldwide to avoid a possible shooting war in the offing. Many Koreans in the Philippines are creating their own Korean towns in key cities where they can do commerce.

The United States already has 28,500 troops in South Korea. It also has F-16 fighter aircraft and A-10 bomber jets. South Korea's military is also very well stocked, with F-35 Fighter Jets, Aegis Destroyers, and all kinds of military hardware purchased from the United States.

The THAAD missile system being erected in a contract with Lockheed-Martin, in cold war terms, is a "strike enabling system." Once the system is completed, the US and South Korean forces that are already in the Peninsula are free to launch an attack on North Korea, China, or Russia. The THAAD system, modeled after Israel's Iron Dome, would prevent retaliation strikes aimed at disabling the attackers. THAAD enables the US and South Korea to begin striking countries in the region, while shielding themselves from any response. Furthermore, THAAD includes a radar system that will closely monitor regional activity, not only in North Korea, but also in northern China.

Its not hard to tell why Russia and China are loudly objecting to this multi-billion dollar military project. Strike enabling systems with penetrating radars are not a mechanism of defusing tension, in an already tense region. THAAD is the latest development in the Pentagon's ongoing "Asian Pivot," moving forces into the Pacific. Similar moves have already escalated tensions in the South China Sea."

The Pentagon's 'Asian Pivot' is still very much in place and has already created an arms race and a modern day cold war producing more tension in the already tense region.

Dr. Erick San Juan, D.Litt.   **46**

Even within South Korea "many Koreans have protested against the completion of the THAAD project. The demonstrators, by and large, are not even subversives nor radicals, but simply patriotic Koreans who believe hostile moves against their Chinese and Russian neighbors do not serve the country's interest. Among opponents is the well-known politician Lee Jae-myung, who is one of the "big three" likely to run in the upcoming Korean presidential election.

Lee Jae-Myung, who wants the US military presence scaled back, is one of the so called "big three" expected to run in the upcoming election. More and more Koreans agree with his argument that allying with the United States against the north, China, and Russia, is not in the people's best interest. Furthermore, less than 4% of the population stands behind the disgraced President Park. South Korea could soon be moving in the same direction as the Philippines, where the long standing neoliberal, pro-American status quo was shaken up by the election of Pres. Rodrigo Duterte.

With the THAAD controversy boiling, amid bribery scandals, impeachment proceedings, discontent with the status quo, and renewed tensions with the North, and ailing economy, the southern half of the Korean peninsula is gradually becoming more and more of a global hotspot. The point of disagreement seems to be about the role southern Korean will play in the world. Will it remain an extension of US influence in Asia, or will the southern half of the Korean peninsula follow in the footsteps of its powerful Chinese neighbors and northern countryfolk? Will Koreans in the south declare their economic, political, and military independence from the United States and Japan?

These questions, which have driven so many uprisings, protests, military coups, and strikes since 1945 are not going away any time soon. (Source: Caleb Maupin, political analyst and activist based in New York)

It seems more and more flashpoints are created due to geopolitical and economic issues between nations in the hottest spot in the world, the Asia-Pacific region and the programmed design of a global war is inevitable and the delay is getting shorter like a ticking bomb.

ooooo

MARCH 8, 2017
In the Brink of War

The world, is in the brink of war as tensions from different parts of the planet occur almost on a regular basis showing off their latest firepower like what North Korea did recently.

"North Korea's launch of four missiles on Monday was a training exercise for a strike on US bases in Japan and was supervised by leader Kim Jong-un, Pyongyang's state media said Tuesday.

Three of the four missiles came down provocatively close to Japan, in waters that are part of its exclusive economic zone, representing a challenge to the US administration. Another was fiund at east asia.

Washington and Tokyo have sought an emergency meeting of the UN Security Council to discuss the launch, likely to be scheduled for Wednesday.

Under UN resolutions, Pyongyang is barred from any use of ballistic missile technology, and the US ambassador to the UN, Nikki Haley, said on Twitter that the world "won't allow" North Korea to continue on its "destructive path55."

But six sets of UN sanctions since its first nuclear test in 2006 have failed to halt Pyongyang's drive for what it insist are defensive weapons.

Kim Jong-un ordered his military "to keep highly alert as required by the grim situation in which an actual war may break out anytime", KCNA reported, and to be ready to "open fire to annihilate the enemies" when ordered." (By Agence France-Presse, March 7, 2017)

The scud missiles fired by North Korea provocatively near Japan and over the Korean Peninsula are clear signs of war provocations which Kim Jong-un said that "an actual war may break out anytime". US allies like Japan and South Korea have reacted strongly against such actions by North Korea :

'This clearly shows North Korea has entered a new stage of threat'—Shinzo Abe, Japan's PM

'The results of the North having a nuclear weapon in its hands will be gruesome beyond imagination' — Hwang Kyo-ahn, South Korea's acting President.

Even Beijing has become increasingly frustrated with Pyongyang's nuclear and missile activities, and last month announced a suspension of all coal imports from the North until the end of the year — a crucial source of foreign currency.

Pyongyang wants to develop an intercontinental ballistic missile capable of reaching the US mainland — something Trump has vowed would not happen.

It has undoubtedly made progress in its efforts in recent years, although questions remain over its ability to master re-entry technology and miniaturize a nuclear weapon sufficiently to fit it onto a missile warhead. (Ibid)

For over a decade since its first nuclear test and sanctions were already given to NoKor by the United Nations, and now this? How come? What happen to UN's sanctions? Questions that have to be addressed soon before an actual war of Kim will materialize.

On the other side of the globe, "Trump's 'Moderate' Defense Secretary Has Already Brought Us to the Brink of War" the title of Mehdi Hasan's article – "Did you know that the Trump administration almost went to war with Iran at the start of February?

Perhaps you were distracted by Gen. Michael Flynn's resignation as national security adviser or by President Trump's online jihad against Nordstrom. Or maybe you missed the story because the New York Times bizarrely buried it in the midst of a long piece on the turmoil and chaos inside the National Security Council.

Defense Secretary James Mattis, according to the paper, wanted the U.S. Navy to "intercept and board an Iranian ship to look for contraband weapons possibly headed to Houthi fighters in Yemen. ... But the ship was in international waters in the Arabian Sea, according to two officials. Mr. Mattis ultimately decided to set the operation aside, at least for now. White House officials said, "that was because news of the impending operation leaked."

Get that? It was only thanks to what Mattis's commander in chief has called "illegal leaks", that the operation was (at least temporarily) set aside and military action between the United States and Iran was averted.

Am I exaggerating? Ask the Iranians. "Boarding an Iranian ship is a shortcut" to confrontation, says Seyyed Hossein Mousavian, former member of Iran's National Security Council and a close ally of Iranian President

Hassan Rouhani. Even if a firefight in international waters were avoided, the Islamic Republic, Mousavian tells me, "would retaliate" and has "many other options for retaliation."

Trita Parsi, head of the National Iranian American Council and author of the forthcoming book "Losing an Enemy — Obama, Iran and the Triumph of Diplomacy," agrees. Such acts of "escalation" by the Trump administration, he tells me, "significantly increases the risk of war."

So why would a retired Marine Corps general such as Mattis be willing to provoke a conflict with Tehran over a single ship? The fact is that Mattis, too, is perceived to be obsessed with Iran. He has hyperbolically called the Islamic Republic "the single most enduring threat to stability and peace in the Middle East" and — in a Trump-esque descent into the world of conspiracy theories — suggested Tehran is working with ISIS. "Iran is not an enemy of ISIS," Mattis declaimed in 2016, because "the one country in the Middle East that has not been attacked" by ISIS "is Iran. That is more than happenstance, I'm sure."

According to the Washington Post, in the run-up to the talks over Iran's nuclear program, "Israelis may have questioned Obama's willingness to use force against Iran. … But they believed Mattis was serious." The general, in his capacity as head of U.S. Central Command, even proposed launching "dead of night" airstrikes on Iranian soil in 2011, in retaliation for Tehran's support for anti-American militias in Iraq — a proposal rejected by White House officials who were worried that it "risked starting yet another war in the Middle East."

Mousavian is puzzled by the defense secretary's hawkishness: "He is one of the most experienced U.S. generals and he knows … the consequences of confrontation with Iran would be tenfold what the U.S. experienced in Afghanistan and Iraq combined."

Mattis allegedly has been tied to some of the worst war crimes of the Iraq invasion. It was he who gave the order to attack the village of Mukaradeeb in April 2004 — a decision he would later admit took him only 30 seconds to approve — which killed 42 civilians, including 13 children, who were attending a wedding there. "I don't have to apologize for the conduct of my men," he told reporters.

Six months later, in November 2004, it was Mattis who planned the Marine assault on Fallujah that reduced that city to rubble, forced 200,000 residents from their homes, and resulted, according to the Red Cross, in at least 800 civilian deaths."

We are all living dangerously that any moment a war may broke out and with the political bickering among our country's 'pulpolitikos', we are really looking for trouble as if nobody is minding the store – again?

Ooooo

MARCH 2, 2017
War Cycle is On

"Territorial disputes, coupled with Beijing's increased militarization of the South China Sea, may sway US policymakers to believe that military conflict with China is inevitable. However, such a conflict is avoidable if the US chooses its policy carefully and implements a strategy that all but eliminates military action." (Source: Michael Brady, Asia Times online)

Yes, it is still avoidable but for how long can the delay be if Beijing is very firm and confident that nothing can stop them for fortifying the disputed areas in the South China Sea. And according to Brady, the main reason for such actions by China are the resources that are found in the SCS.

The South China Sea is rich with natural resources. According to the US Geological Survey, 11 billion barrels of oil and 190 trillion cubic feet of natural gas can be found in the hotly disputed region. The Chinese, however, indicate the area may hold more than 200 billion barrels of oil and up to 750 trillion cubic feet of natural gas. Regardless of the exact quantity, these estimates are the primary reason Beijing continues to assert its claim over the region. For China to continue its economic initiatives, unrestricted access to oil and gas remains a national priority.

In addition, 12% of the world's fish catch is in the South China Sea. Since China consumes about 25% of all seafood globally, it's no wonder it continues to claim vast swaths of the region and insists its fisherman have the right to catch there."

So if these vast resources will feed the entire population of China for years to come, the comments of Tillerson and Bannon will make China angry.

What was not told in public were the rare earth metals newly found in the Philippines like Palladium, etc. plus the vast natural gas reserve at Benham Rise near the Pacific.

"At a recent US Senate confirmation hearing, now Secretary of State Rex Tillerson stated: "We're going to have to send China a clear signal that, first, the island-building stops. And second, your access to those islands also is not going to be allowed." Tillerson's comment clearly indicate that President Donald Trump and his administration are willing to use military force if Chinese activities continue. This comment is similar in tone to Steve Bannon's during a podcast in March 2016 when he stated, "We're going to war in the South China Sea in five to 10 years." (Bannon is now senior adviser to President Trump.)

Trump and his national-security team need to understand that China's claim are primarily driven by the need for resources, not sovereignty. According to recent reports, China's population will reach approximately 1.4 billion by 2020. As China's population continues to increase, demand for resources such as fisheries and oil will rise. China's inability to feed its population in the future may ultimately lead to conflict, with or without US intervention." (Ibid)

If it's going to be the US alone that can stop China for grabbing territories in order to take resources to sustain its growing population then so it be. A need that is very basic to humanity but China should also consider the needs of its neighbors so that it will be a win-win solution to every nation in the region.

For Prof. Richard Javad Heydarian's observation, he writes : "US-China rivalry in the South China Sea is ringing alarm bells in littoral Southeast Asian nations, with fears rising that Donald Trump's administration could tilt the region's delicate balance towards conflict.

China has recently expanded its strategic footprint on various disputed features, deploying new weapons systems and establishing advanced military facilities on artificially reclaimed islands in both the Spratly and Paracel chains.

Trump's administration has indicated it views China's action as a direct challenge to freedom of navigation and overflight in one of the world's most important sea lines of trade and communications, and a challenge to American strategic primacy in the Western Pacific.

US Secretary of State Rex Tillerson suggested during his confirmation hearing that the US could impose a naval blockade on China's artificial islands in the Spratlys. The threat was followed by this week's deployment of the aircraft carrier USS Carl Vinson to the South China Sea as part of so-called "routine operations" in the area.

Washington's deployment of the USS Carl Vinson, accompanied by an armada of warships, was a clear signal that neither will America sit by idly as the strategic balance shifts. The last time America showed such force in the South China Sea was in early 2016, when there were concerns of imminent Chinese reclamation activity on the Philippine-claimed Scarborough Shoal.

That was under the pro-US Philippine President Benigno Aquino administration, which was replaced last July by the at least outwardly more China-friendly Duterte. China's growing military prowess, its putting pressure on America to develop a stronger naval presence in the region, with power projection capabilities at nearby bases, particularly at Subic and Oyster Bay in the Philippines.

But without stronger engagement and clearer messaging under Trump, it is not clear if those or other regional facilities will be available when America most needs them."

Not only under US President Donald Trump that should have clearer messaging but most especially our very own President Rody Duterte, because our country can be used by China as its springboard in accomplishing its claim in the SCS and Taiwan in the process to achieve Pres. Xi Jinping's China dream. The current administration of Pres. Duterte allowed it in his belief and in order to avoid conflict for obvious reason that we don't have the capability to go to war with China.

In order not to tilt the balance towards creating a regional conflict that may end up into a global war in the process, leaders of nation and all the other stakeholders should sit down and talk, after all diplomacy should be on the top of the list to straighten up misunderstandings. In so doing miscalculation will be avoided.

But the Chinese missiles being deployed in the nearby reefs and the perceived war cycle is on and predicted to go all hell by the third quarter of this year is really worrisome.

May God forbid!

ooooo

FEBRUARY 22, 2017
Drug Cartel, Who's Behind?

"Transnational criminal organizations and subsidiary organizations, including transnational drug cartels, have spread throughout the nation, threatening the safety of the United States and its citizens.... These groups are drivers of crime, corruption, violence, and misery.... In particular, the trafficking by cartels of controlled substances has triggered a resurgence in deadly drug abuse and a corresponding rise in violent crime related to drugs.... A comprehensive and decisive approach is required to dismantle these organized crime syndicates and restore safety for the American people."

This is US President Donald Trump's executive order of February 9 which is powerful and clear on his war on drugs.

Trump noted that he had brought a number of law enforcement officials to the White House, and asked them:

"what impact do drugs have in terms of a percentage on crime? They said, 75 to 80 percent. That's pretty sad. We're going to stop the drugs from pouring in. We're going to stop those drugs from poisoning our youth, from poisoning our people. We're going to be ruthless in that fight. We have no choice.... And we're going to take that fight to the drug cartels and work to liberate our communities from their terrible grip of violence."

The proliferation of illegal drugs obviously reached the mighty land of Uncle Sam and the newly elected US president Trump, like our own President Rody Duterte will make sure that their citizens are protected against the poisonous impact of drugs.

In the article of Mike Billington of the Executive Intelligence Review (EIR) – 'Trump Launches War on Drugs, But Must Target Drug Banks' clearly states that the international banking system has tolerated the transnational shipment of illegal drugs across continents.

"The one problem with the Trump War on Drugs — and a potential Achilles Heel if not corrected — is the failure to identify and target the actual core of the international drug cartel — the banks which facilitate this business. The publication by EIR in 1978 of the first edition of Dope, Inc., and the subsequent editions of that blockbuster expose, documented in great detail how the illicit drug business — the biggest business in the world — is reportedly controlled entirely by the west and Wall Street banks, since the time of the British Opium Wars against China, and continuing through to today.

The identification of the "too-big-to-fail" banks in London and New York as the headquarters of Dope Inc., will also provide yet another motivation for the immediate restoration of Glass Steagall, to stop the criminal money laundering and speculation which has brought the trans-Atlantic financial system to ruin.

In 2009, after the 2008 near-collapse of the western banking system, Antonio Maria Costa, then the head of the UN office on drugs and crime, identified the fact that the international banks had become "drug dependent." He said:

"In many instances, the money from drugs was the only liquid investment capital. In the second half of 2008, liquidity was the banking system's main problem and hence liquid capital became an important factor. Inter-bank loans were funded by money that originated from the drugs trade and other illegal activities... There were signs that some banks were rescued that way."

Viktor Ivanov, the Director of the Russian Federal Narcotics Service from 2008 until 2016, speaking in Washington in 2011, said: In order to shut this down, "Drug money and global drug trafficking are actually not just valuable elements of, but as donors of scarce liquidity, a vital and indispensable segment of the whole monetary system."

Russia and the United States must work in tandem, Ivanov said, to effect a "drastic transformation of the international financial system.... To a certain extent, we are observing a revival of the logic of the Glass-Steagall Act, adopted in the U.S. in 1933 at the height of the Great Depression, which separated the deposit and investment functions of banks."

With the advancement of technology through the internet every transaction of drug money can be done fast and hard to trace.

Just the same in our case, the transhipment of drugs through our waterways because of our vast coastline, and the possibility of the presence of some Chinese in our Coast Guard, drugs come and go without any fuss.

I hope that the recent agreement between coast guards of China and the Philippines to stop sea bandits like Abu Sayyaf's will also be of help in stopping the transport of illegal drugs and its raw materials.

The perception is that even by air, sea, land and the virtual cyberworld, proliferation of drugs will continue because of the presence of corrupt people in the government. The worst, narco financiers and politicians now control many nations worldwide.

Just like in the movies, now its reality.

ooooo

FEBRUARY 15, 2017
Tensions Will Continue in the Pacific Rim

War rhetoric between the U.S. and China is finally starting to cool down. The title of an article by James Holbrooks (TheAntiMedia.org) posted at True Activist (Feb. 7) but is it really cooling down?

Holbrooks based the said situation when Secretary of Defense James Mattis suggested the hotly disputed issue of the South China Sea should be handled diplomatically rather than through warfare. Yes, a very comforting statement in the midst of tensions in the East and South China Sea.

Calling the defense secretary's words a "mind-soothing pill" that "dispersed the clouds of war that many feared were gathering over the South China Sea," the China Daily hinted at a warning in U.S.-China relations.

"Mattis has inspired optimism here that things may not be as bad as previously portrayed," the state-controlled newspaper wrote.

Although in reality things are not as mind-soothing as it seems. As the article continues: "In fact, even as James Mattis was suggesting over the weekend that between the U.S. and China, the diplomatic road was the one to take on the issue of territorial sovereignty, he was also accusing the Asian superpower of using coercion to force its will upon neighboring countries.

"We have watched in the South China Sea as China has shredded the trust of nations in the region," Mattis said at the conference in Tokyo, "apparently trying to have veto authority over security and economic conditions of neighboring states."

Providing further evidence that tensions are invariably rising between China and the United States — despite what government officials on both sides might happen to say at a given time — Fox News reported Monday that three Chinese warships have just sailed into the East China Sea.

It would be difficult to argue the timing is coincidental, as just two days before, the U.S. solidified its security commitments to ally Japan. And those commitments essentially back up the claim that Japan — not China — has a sovereign claim to the contested Senkaku Islands in the East China Sea.

In effect, it's the same fundamental disagreement over two different bodies of water — both of which are in one region. And it's a region neither the United States nor China appears willing to cede control over."

That is the crucial point of finding ways to really avoid an impending war between the US and China – the control over contested territories in the region. In both cases - the East and South China Sea, the nations involved are both allies of the US, namely Japan and the Philippines.

The war rhetoric may cool down for a while but the tensions will continue. Even our own President Rodrigo Duterte said several times that the moment will come, in his term, that our country and China will sit down and will discuss the arbitration body's ruling that favored our country. Whether China will like it or not, the said ruling from The Hague should be honored to give way to a lasting peace in the region and not just a piecemeal.

It is quite obvious that it is not only China's needs that has to be addressed when it comes to natural resources which is in abundance in the contested area in the South China Sea by fortifying the reclaimed areas militarily by China. There is no way for our country to have the chance of extracting oil, gas and other minerals that will also supply our growing needs and be used for our development.

That is the gist of the article by Gregory Poling – Prepare for A Stormy 2017 in the South China Sea - The number of Chinese naval, coast guard, and paramilitary vessels in the area will continue to grow as facilities at the three large artificial islands allow Chinese assets to consistently patrol the southern reaches of the nine-dash line as never before. China also continues to construct sophisticated radar and signals intelligence capabilities, bolstering its ability to monitor and intercept vessels anywhere in the area, and advanced anti-aircraft and anti-missile point defenses to protect these new power projection capabilities.

The desire to see Chinese diplomatic softening as a sign of a new status quo is understandable, and it is important that the door be left open for Beijing to deescalate. But China's recent behavior should be seen as the best indicator of its future intentions. Beijing has accomplished its short-term goal of avoiding widespread censure after the July ruling. But it made no effort to clarify its claims or slowdown military construction, which would have suggested a more long-term commitment to peacefully resolve disputes. It is therefore only reasonable to assume that China continues to seek dominance throughout the nine-dash line, by coercion when necessary. Unlike the Philippines and Malaysia, other countries with a stake in the South China Sea recognize this and are preparing for heightened tensions as China makes use of its new facilities. The incoming U.S. administration will need to do the same, because the next crisis is likely just a matter of time."

We should be wary of the pressure for President Rody Duterte to implement a revolutionary government as per instigation of a self proclaimed local CIA laying the predicate. He thought he may get what he wish for at our expense.

ooooo

FEBRUARY 6, 2017
Imminent War in the Offing

Is war between the US and China imminent as what Steve Bannon, who is President Donald Trump's chief political strategist said last March?

According to Steve Bannon the United States will go to war with China in "five to 10 years" over the South China Sea dispute.

The said comments resurfaced at a time when Washington and Beijing's relations have soured after Trump questioned the "One China" policy and Secretary of State Rex Tillerson said China should be barred from islands in the contested region.

"We're going to war in the South China Sea in five to 10 years, aren't we? There's no doubt about that. They're taking their sandbars and making basically stationary aircraft carriers and putting missiles on those. They come here to the United States in front of our face — and you understand how important face is — and say it's an ancient territorial sea," Bannon said on a radio show hosted for Breitbart in March 2016. (Source: Vishakha Sonawane at IBT online)

US President Donald Trump even before his inauguration released some pronouncements that are not pleasant to China's ears. One of these very hot issues is the One China Policy – "A state-run Chinese newspaper warned Sunday that Beijing will take "revenge" if the United States abandons the "one China" policy under Donald Trump's administration. The comments came after Taiwanese President Tsai Ing-wen made a stopover in Houston.

"Trump is yet to be inaugurated, and there is no need for Beijing to sacrifice bilateral ties for the sake of Taiwan. But in case he tears up the one-China policy after taking office, the mainland is fully prepared," the Global

Times said in an editorial. "Beijing would rather break ties with the US if necessary. We would like to see whether US voters will support their president to ruin Sino-US relations and destabilize the entire Asia-Pacific region."

"If Trump reneges on the one-China policy after taking office, the Chinese people will demand the government to take revenge. There is no room for bargaining," the newspaper warned.

"Under the 'one China' policy, there is only a single state called 'China' despite there being two governments. People's Republic of China, popularly known as the mainland China, considers Taiwan (officially known as Republic of China) a renegade province. However, Taiwan considers itself an independent country. Both PRC and Taiwan claim to be the lawful government of one China, but in reality, Taiwan has control only over a few small islands."

"Sticking to [the one China] principle is not a capricious request by China upon US presidents, but an obligation of US presidents to maintain China-US relations and respect the existing order of the Asia-Pacific," the Global Times said.

In its editorial, the Global Times also said that China "will impose further military pressure" on Taiwan and "Tsai needs to face the consequences for every provocative step she takes." (Vishakha Sonawane for IBT)

Like a programmed scenario, delays can happen but it will happen and the US-Sino relations is not getting any better.

In his article China Jockeying for Position in South China Sea, Larry Edelson writes, "Hullabaloo over President Trump's policies, his nationalist stance and fears over potential trade conflicts may have turned some investors' focus away from numerous geopolitical hotspots.

But not mine.

In fact, these hotspots are going to get worse before they get better ... and they play right into my larger War Cycle research."

Take for example the latest – and frankly stealthy developments – growing from the budding romance between China and the Philippines.

No question this duo has experienced their share of conflict – but that's changing. Especially as China contemplates its military ambitions and the Philippines' strategic location in the South China Sea. Plus, it's no secret that the Philippines' populist President Rodrigo Duterte is open to a new relationship with China.

Let's Make a Deal

In late January, China made good on an initial $3.7 billion investment (part of a $24 billion deal) to aid the Philippines in numerous infrastructure projects. The investment represents a massive 75% of total foreign investment into the Philippines throughout 2015 ($4.9 billion).

And you can be certain this investment is not a philanthropic exercise to help their neighbor.

From my lens, China's maneuvering is to gain naval access beyond the first island chain and ultimately station military assets at a strategic location in the Pacific.

Complications

The U.S. has a defense treaty with the Philippines, allowing U.S. warships to move freely from the Pacific to Middle East war zones in return for U.S. defense.

But that's in jeopardy after the U.S. didn't adequately come to the Philippines' defense when China took control of Scarborough Shoal and other islands. And that's territory that China is now building runways and stationing missile batteries on.

Meanwhile, China's late 2016 seizure of an American underwater surveillance drone in the region underscores the tense and volatile relationship.

The conflict is further aggravated by comments from newly appointed U.S. Secretary of State Rex Tillerson regarding tensions in the South China Sea: "We're going to send China a clear signal that … island-building stops and access to those islands is not going to be allowed."

Wow. Talk about a South Pacific powder keg."

Indeed a powder keg waiting for an event that can ignite it to a real shooting war. Which reminds us all to be ever vigilant and supportive of our president's correct policies to avoid another war not of our liking and definitely not to be used again as cannon fodder in the process.

The war cycle is on. Most nations in the know are all preparing for it especially big powers with overheating economy involved in the military industrial complex. Let's all be vigilant!

ooooo

JANUARY 31, 2017
China's Masterstroke

The Manila Times news report quoted Professor Renato de Castro of De La Salle University's international studies department as saying in a forum in Makati City, "Foreign policy has to be democratic. It has to reflect the sentiment of the people."

Just like what the recent survey of Pulse Asia revealed that 8 out of 10 Filipinos or 84 percent want the government to assert Philippine rights over the West Philippine Sea. Another aspect of what the Duterte administration should consider, not just plain independent foreign policy. Yes, independent decision with no foreign influence. But it is another thing when you say it should be influenced by the Filipino people – your constituents. Not just you or the people in your loop.

If an overwhelming 84 percent of Filipinos want the government to uphold our rights to the contested area in the South China Sea/West Philippine Sea, it could mean a more aggressive and firm stand to claim it based on the ruling at The Hague's Permanent Court of Arbitration. So, there seems to be a sort of apprehension on the part of the present leadership in pursuing our rightful claim. Why is this so?

It should be noted that this is not new when one is dealing with China economically like in other countries. An article by Brahma Chellaney from the Strategist online explains this further – "If there is one thing at which China's leaders truly excel, it is the use of economic tools to advance their country's geostrategic interests.

Through its $1 trillion 'one belt, one road' initiative, China is supporting infrastructure projects in strategically located developing countries, often by extending huge loans to their governments. As a result, countries are becoming ensnared in a debt trap that leaves them vulnerable to China's influence.

Of course, extending loans for infrastructure projects is not inherently bad. But the projects that China is supporting are often intended not to support the local economy, but to facilitate Chinese access to natural resources, or to open the market for low-cost and shoddy

Chinese goods. In many cases, China even sends its own construction workers, minimizing the number of local jobs that are created. Remember the shady North Rail project?

Several of the projects that have been completed are now bleeding money. For example, Sri Lanka's Mattala Rajapaksa International Airport, which opened in 2013 near Hambantota, has been dubbed the world's emptiest.

Likewise, Hambantota's Magampura Mahinda Rajapaksa Port remains largely idle, as does the multibillion-dollar Gwadar port in Pakistan. For China, however, these projects are operating exactly as needed: Chinese attack submarines have twice docked at Sri Lankan ports, and two Chinese warships were recently pressed into service for Gwadar port security.

In a sense, it is even better for China that the projects don't do well. After all, the heavier the debt burden on smaller countries, the greater China's own leverage becomes. Already, China has used its clout to push Cambodia, Laos, Myanmar, and Thailand to block a united ASEAN stand against China's aggressive pursuit of its territorial claims in the South China Sea."

And that includes our country as the host of the ASEAN summit where the South China Sea issue is not in the agenda.

"Moreover, some countries, overwhelmed by their debts to China, are being forced to sell to it stakes in Chinese-financed projects or hand over their management to Chinese state-owned firms.

In financially risky countries, China now demands majority ownership up front. For example, China clinched a deal with Nepal this month to build another largely Chinese-owned dam there, with its state-run China Three Gorges Corporation taking a 75% stake."

Another crucial issue that may affect national security matters that we already entered into with China, is our electric power grid. Unfortunately, it is not national as the name of the office implies National Grid Corporation of the Philippines and disguised as not wholly owned by the Philippines but partly owned by the state grid of China.

And still many more agreements with China already in the pipeline as what President Rodrigo Duterte proudly told the Filipino nation. And these are not for free, that is what China termed as soft loan, which they are using soft power to entice nations.

And lastly, why is the biggest (so far) rehabilitation center in the world for drug users is located inside a military camp that is financed and built by China's "philanthropist". Did we make a due diligence about Rulin who was rumored to be an underworld character in Binondo during the time of Marcos who hastily left for China according to CANU (PC-INP Constabulary Anti-Narcotic Unit of the late Gen. Bienvenido Felix) retired operatives?

Here is what Brahma Chellaney's warning "by integrating its foreign, economic, and security policies, China is advancing its goal of fashioning a hegemonic sphere of trade, communication, transportation, and security links. If states are saddled with onerous levels of debt as a result, their financial woes only aid China's neocolonial designs. Countries that are not yet ensnared in China's debt trap should take note—and take whatever steps they can to avoid it."

I hope that our economic managers who went to China recently were not caught in the trap.

Just asking...

ooooo

JANUARY 24, 2017
Word War No More?

Beijing on Friday—the 13th no less—threatened the United States with "large-scale war." "Prepare for a military clash" said the Global Times in an editorial.

Beijing was hitting back hard against remarks made by Rex Tillerson, Donald Trump's pick for secretary of State, in his confirmation hearing. "We're going to have to send China a clear signal that, first, the island-building stops and, second, your access to those islands is also not going to be allowed," he told the Senate Foreign Relations Committee Wednesday (January 11).

The nominee also said China's militarizing the islands is "akin to Russia's taking of Crimea."

Observers gasped at Tillerson's words, which signaled a radical change in American policy toward China. Yet his general approach toward Beijing, despite all the criticism he has attracted in the last few days, is the correct one for these times." (Source: The Daily Beast, Gordon G. Chang 1.16.2017)

Is it really the right approach towards China's claim in the South China Sea, confrontational rather than diplomacy?

Analysts said Tillerson's testimony, combined with his future boss's earlier pronouncements, signaled that a Trump administration is poised to take a much tougher stance on China.

Since winning the election, Trump has lashed out at China on Twitter, made clear he's serious about wringing a new trade deal from Beijing and upended US policy toward Taiwan -- an issue of deep sensitivity for China.

"All the quotes taken together do signal that, like Trump and some of his advisers, are poised to take much firmer stance on China in the South China Sea and across the board," said Ashley Townshend, a research fellow, at the United States Studies Centre at the University of Sydney.

But Townshend doubted whether Tillerson would really follow through on some of the specifics of his testimony.

"The US cannot block China's access to the islands without causing a confrontation, probably a military confrontation, and it would be illegal for the US to block access to the vast majority of those islands and reefs," he said. (Source: Tillerson sets stage for showdown with Beijing over South China Sea by Katie Hunt, CNN, 1.13.17)

Most likely a regional conflict will erupt once US under Trump regime will implement such blockade to stop China's access to the reclaimed islands in the SCS. And what will be the stand of our country if ever a confrontation will occur?

RP must avoid the prospect of entanglement. A sound advice from businessman Manny Lopez in his analysis - A geopolitical scenario wherein an ultimatum from the US and its allies to stop the development and militarization of artificial islands in SCS being rejected by China is highly probable. Initially, a limited Air-Sea battle between the dominant and rising power to test their resolve will happen either by accident or localized decision, unless reason and skillful diplomacy prevails pre-emptively. The Republic of the Philippines must avoid entanglements in the superpower conflict by intelligently pursuing an independent and neutral foreign policy. We must not allow our shores to become the staging ground of the war effort by either side. However, we must continue to positively engage both superpowers and offer win-win solutions to help resolve the upcoming conflict and save ourselves.

China's expected refusal to dismantle its air-defense and anti-ship missile systems deployed in the 7 artificial islands in SCS could be a compelling reason for the US Navy to attack using submarine-launched Harpoons and ship-borne Tomahawk cruise missiles to eliminate the said installations from a safe distance. Freedom of navigation in the South China Sea is perceived to be crucial to ensure unhampered trade in the busy shipping route, where more than US$ 5-Trillion worth of goods transits each year. At least a couple of US carrier battle groups supported by Japanese, Australian and South Korean navies will likely be deployed in the area to effect control of the sea lanes. How the Russian and Indian Navies will play their role in the inevitable conflict is yet to be determined."

As an observer of events as they unfold, we have been writing (and speaking in our daily radio broadcast) that we must not allow the use of our territories as the battleground for another conflict in the region and much more – not to drag our country and people to an unnecessary war in the process.

With the new leadership in the US, we are in for some surprising times. Finally, the administration that will threaten the "great wall of sand" in the SCS and might give Xi some second thoughts of changing his foreign policy was leaked by the Bloomberg News Tuesday January 24,2017 and published by Businessmirror.

"Confronted by the challenge of a Donald J. Trump led White House, China is signaling it's ready to work with the new administration and has already taken a handful of policy steps that may help fend off criticism over access to its markets."

But it's not all olive branch, Xinhua news article congratulating Trump also laid out the areas China regards as off limits. It said, "China's resolve to safeguard it's defining interests in Taiwan and the South China Sea islands has always been strong."

Xi allegedly has a strong domestic imperative not to appear weak before a twice a decade Communist party congress when several top leaders are due to be replaced except himself?

Ooooo

JANUARY 17, 2017
Manna from Heaven

The following are the words of President Rodrigo Duterte before a gathering of envoys at the New Year Vin D'Honneur at Malacañang.

"In a world that recognizes our interconnectedness and respect each others' sovereign independence, the horizons and frontiers of cooperation are virtually limitless. Friendship, after all, knows no bound."

"We value partners as we seek to strengthen existing friendships even as we pursue new ones."

"We believe that friends help each other and utilize constructive engagement to achieve common goals. In truth, we all share the same aspiration of greater peace, progress, and prosperity."

I'm sure that with these statements of our president, a lot of people will agree and not only the Filipinos but most especially the world leaders because interdependence among nations is beyond political-economy but mutual respect in each others sovereignty as individual nation-states.

With this outlook from President Duterte, in relation to the community of nations, he is on the right track and this shows when Japan Prime Minister Shinzo Abe arrived in the country recently and pledged "Official Development Assistance and private sector investments which, together, will be in the order of one trillion yen ($8.7 billion) over the next five years."

The partnership for development among Asian neighbors is a healthy way of resolving issues and with PM Abe and their grant assistance to combat terrorism and piracy by a grant of $5.2 million for Philippine coast guard speedboats and anti-terrorism equipment.

It is just like a very timely 'manna' from heaven. Especially now that the Duterte administration is fighting several fronts, both domestic and international, with the plunging peso, needed foreign loans to sustain the government operation. War on drugs which invite the fear of the unknown why many believe is the reason why Pres. Digong has been talking about Martial law which several surveys say will not be accepted by the people and by congress. Rumor mill is talking about a revolutionary government but where is PRRD's forces will come from?

Japan already contributes heavily to the largely impoverished Philippines through the Manila-based Asian Development Bank, which has lent the Philippines an average $745 million per year since 2006 for poverty reduction.

With the Duterte administration, the country is hoping that the funds will go to the intended projects sans corruption.

Like the Philippines, Japan also has territorial issues with China in the East China Sea but Abe, however, said "the issue of the South China Sea is linked directly to regional peace and stability and is a concern to the entire international community."

His two-day visit to Manila aims to further solidify relations with the Philippines at a time when Duterte is cozying up to China and Russia while taking a hostile stance toward Tokyo's main ally, the United States. Japan is among the top trading partners of the Philippines and one of its largest aid providers. Thanks God for the blessings coming from Japan.

With Japan Prime Minister's support to Duterte's leadership, many hopes that this will avert a programmed bloody civil war or Xi Jinping's China 'dream' to annex Taiwan and the Philippines in the process.

The mere fact that a survey of 1,200 adult respondents nationwide between December 6 to 11 (had a margin of error of plus or minus 3 percent) found 76 percent of adult Filipinos trust the U.S. while 70 percent expressed trust for Japan. Sixty-one percent said they lacked trust in China and 58 percent distrust Russia.

Even if we don't rely much on surveys and always take it with a grain of salt so to speak, in this crucial time Pres. Duterte only needs to unite the nation and have peace and prosperity as his living legacy. We have to support his righteous advocacy. No need for a China or communist inspired revolutionary government which is a prescription for MAD - a mutually assured destruction.

Dr. Erick San Juan, D.Litt.   **68**

Let us keep on DOING GOOD BEING GOOD and FEEL GOOD! God bless the Philippines!
(Note: Sources from various news network online.)

ooooo

JANUARY 10, 2017
Prepare for the Worst

Predictions for 2017 – Year of the Fire Rooster, don't bode well for China. Although the Fire Rooster is the sign of dawn and awakening, it is said, "The union of the Fire elements with the Rooster's Metal during 2017 will create great tensions, this will create an electric atmosphere that will intensify the actions of the leaders of several nations and in the economies that will generate even more deterioration in the political climate. Further migration is thought to be caused by strong wars and climate change. It is predicted that some governments will take a tough line of mandate, there will be a lot of authoritarianism and there will be many threats of various kinds that could be the cause of more clashes between nations." (Source: China's colonization of the Philippines by Perry Diaz)

Is this the reason why 2017 could be the year of the next global war based on the Chinese calendar and most probably Pres. Xi Jinping of China will start it? What could be the driving force that might start another war? Just asking.

In my past article where I tackled the Chinese Dream that will be the force to push Xi to make China great again, here is what Perry Diaz said in his article – "When Xi Jinping came to power in 2012, he immediately pursued his "Chinese Dream," which is the revival of imperial China that had maintained Chinese hegemony in Asia during the reign of the Ming Dynasty. "The great revival of the Chinese nation is the greatest Chinese Dream," Xi said before taking office.

Two years later, China started building seven artificial islands on top of reefs and shoals in the Spratly archipelago. Upon completion, the Chinese built airfields that could accommodate large aircraft and deep harbors where Chinese warships could dock.

With the militarization of these islands, which are less than 200 miles away from the province of Palawan, Chinese forces are now at the doorsteps of the Philippines ready to strike when the time is ripe."

Unfortunately this year might be ripe enough to annex the Philippines and Taiwan. Strategic analysts believe that China needs an external war to unite the Chinese people as Xi tries desperately to stay in power while the unhappy members of the Chinese Politburo tries to replace him.

"The weakening of China's economy and its increasing belligerence are occurring in tandem, and the progression from one to the other appears to be related. For one thing, a deteriorating economy will undermine Xi Jinping's bold efforts to consolidate power, and the resulting disunity will surely make China's external posture unpredictable.

The country could turn inward, but lashing out looks more probable, especially if Chinese leaders think the decline in the economy will close a window of opportunity to achieve historic goals, like enlargement of Chinese control over neighboring lands and peripheral seas.

China's economy is moving in wrong directions. In many ways, the rest of the world is bound to suffer as a result." (Source: Is China's Economy Past the Point of No Return? By Gordon G. Chang)

We should be wary and help the Duterte administration realize that getting too close to China is not a good idea and will only put us all in danger of a possible annexation of China. Pres. Duterte seems gypped to believe that the biggest threat to his post is his Vice president Leni Robredo and the 'yellows'. He has to review the movie, "Star Wars3", to realize his predicament. Plus Bongbong Marcos is itching to replace VP Leni, prelude in getting Malacanang as leverage to global bankers and other country claimants to their not so hidden loot kept at British Virgin Islands as exposed by Panama Papers.

And as what I have been warning of the presence of sleepers here, Perry writes "according to a reliable source in Manila, most of the Chinoys (short for Chinese-Filipinos) are patriotic and loyal to the Philippine flag. However, some of them are believed to be pro-China "sleepers" ready to act when called upon by their PLA handlers. Some of them are sons of rich ethnic Taipans who sent them to China to study. Allegedly, some of them took PLA officer's training. It is also alleged that units of the PLA have already infiltrated the country posing as investors, casino operators and worst Chinese Triad underworld boss.

It is interesting to note that prior to the outbreak of World War II, thousands of Japanese nationals were working in the Philippines. Many of them were sleepers and once war broke out, they put on their military uniforms and joined the invading Japanese forces.

Meanwhile, the anti-communist forces in the Philippines have organized themselves as the "Save Our Soldier" Movement. Interestingly, the acronym for "Save Our Soldier" is SOS, which is the international code signal of extreme distress and an urgent appeal for help. The question is: Is the SOS Movement poised and ready to act if Duterte forms a pro-communist revolutionary government? One can only surmise that the probability increased due to recent confluence of events."

A very dangerous and frightening scenario that we hope will not happen. God help us.

ooooo

JANUARY 3, 2017
Chess Game

Both leaders are polar opposites – a mensch in Moscow on the right side of history compared to a US menace in Washington waging war on humanity. [Mensch means a person of dignity and honor. See: https://en.wikipedia.org/wiki/Mensch]

A paragraph taken from the article of Stephen Lendman referring to Russia's President Vladimir Putin and US outgoing president Barack Obama on the recent sanctions granted to Russian diplomats in the US by Obama for the alleged cyber attacks on the recent US elections.

What Is The Obama Regime Up To? A title/question of Paul Craig Roberts' article which he writes

"Obama has announced new sanctions on Russia based on unsubstantiated charges by the CIA that the Russian government influenced the outcome of the US presidential election with "malicious cyber-enabled activities."

The US Department of Homeland Security (DHS) has issued a report "related to the declaration of 35 Russian officials persona non grata for malicious cyber activity and harassment."

The report is a description of "tools and infrastructure used by Russian intelligence services to compromise and exploit networks and infrastructure associated with the recent U.S. election, as well as a range of U.S. government, political and private sector entities."

The 'paper' does not provide any evidence that the tools and infrastructure were used to influence the outcome of the US presidential election. It is simply a description of what is said to be Russian capabilities.

Moreover, the said information begins with this statement: "DISCLAIMER: This report is provided 'as is' for informational purposes only. The Department of Homeland Security (DHS) does not provide any warranties of any kind regarding any information contained within."

In other words, the report not only provides no evidence of the use of the Russian tools and infrastructure in order to influence the US presidential election, the report will not even warrant the correctness of its description of Russian capabilities.

Thus the DHS report makes it completely clear that the Obama regime has no evidential basis for its allegations on the basis of which it has imposed more sanctions on Russia.

A top adviser to Pres.-elect Donald Trump, former CIA director James Woolsey and now an adviser of Trump on national security issues told CNN's Jim Sciutto that determining who was behind the hacks is difficult but he believes the Russian and possibly others were involved.(www.cnn.com)

What is going on here?

First there is the question of the legality of the sanctions even if there were evidence. I am not certain, but I think that sanctions require the action of a body, such as the UN Security Council, and cannot legally be imposed unilaterally by one country.

Additionally, it is unclear why Obama is calling the expulsion of Russian diplomats "sanctions." No other country has to do likewise. During the Cold War when diplomats were expelled for spying, it was not called "sanctions." Sanctions imply more than unilateral or bilateral expulsions of diplomats.

Second, it is clear that Obama, the US intelligence agencies and the New York Times are fully aware that the allegation is false. It is also clear that if the Intel agency actually believes the allegation, the intelligence agency is perceived as incompetent and cannot be believed on any subject.

Third, President Trump can rescind the sanctions in 21 days, a third reason that the sanctions are ridiculous.

So why are President Obama, the 'Agency' and the New York Times making charges that they know are false and for which they have not produced a shred of evidence? http://www.nytimes.com/2016/12/29/opinion/president-obama-punishes-russia-at-last.html?_r=1

One obvious answer is that the neoconized Obama regime is desperate to ruin US-Russian relations past the point that Trump can repair them. As the New York Times puts it, "Mr. Obama's actions clearly create a problem for Mr. Trump." The question the New York Times says, is whether Trump "stands with his democratic allies on Capitol Hill or his authoritarian friend in the Kremlin."

Although the exiting Obama has given the said sanctions, Russia did not retaliate – verbally.

"In response to Obama's new sanctions, a same day article quoted Sergey Lavrov, saying Russia "cannot leave unanswered insults of the kind, reciprocity is the law of diplomacy and foreign relations."

He recommended Putin respond tit for tat while blasting Obama's deplorable action. It seemed certain, but didn't happen. Putin took the high ground, in stark contrast to his disgraceful US counterpart, issuing a statement, saying:

"We regard the recent unfriendly steps taken by the outgoing US administration as provocative and aimed at further weakening the Russia-US relationship."

"This runs contrary to the fundamental interests of both the Russian and American people. Considering the global security responsibilities of Russia and the United

States, this is also damaging to international relations as a whole."

"As it proceeds from international practice, Russia has reasons to respond in kind. Although we have the right to retaliate, we will not resort to irresponsible 'kitchen' diplomacy but will plan our further steps to restore Russian-US relations based on the policies of the Trump Administration."

Actually according to Joe Uchill of thehill.com, Russian Central Bank was hacked last December for $31 million. The Russian FSB and SVR RF, the external intelligence agencies could make the blame game and say it was the American hackers and there's a plan to destabilize Russian financial system.

But Putin resisted to react that way and said-

"The diplomats who are returning to Russia will spend the New Year's holidays with their families and friends. We will not create any problems for US diplomats."

"We will not expel anyone. We will not prevent their families and children from using their traditional leisure sites during the New Year's holidays."

"Moreover, I invite all children of US diplomats accredited in Russia to the New Year and Christmas children's parties in the Kremlin." [The Russian Orthodox Church uses the old Julian calendar for religious holidays, which puts Christmas on January 7.]

"It is regrettable that the Obama Administration is ending its term in this manner. Nevertheless, I offer my New Year greetings to President Obama and his family."

"My season's greetings also to President-elect Donald Trump and the American people."

"I wish all of you happiness and prosperity."

For the final comment – "Russian Foreign Ministry spokeswoman Maria Zakharova explained that Obama's expulsion order disrupts the lives of 96 Russian nationals – 35 diplomats and family members.

Some targeted diplomats only arrived in America two months ago. "It is not clear how they could have participated in (alleged) activities that, according to the secret services, took place in the spring of 2016," Zakharova explained.

The left US January 1, Obama's happy new year greeting.

There might be more to Obama's provocation than meets the eye. (Source: Putin's Response to Obama's New Sanctions by Stephen Lendman, 12/30/16)

Will the Russia-US relations continue to be in such state of harsh diplomacy under the Trump administration? Who will control the next administration's foreign policy? The CFR, the neocons or the hidden hands of the globalists in order to start the programmed crisis and begin another global war?

Lets be vigilant!

ooooo

DECEMBER 27, 2016
Spilling The Beans

Certain issues with the US verbalized in a not so nice way by President Rody Duterte plus his name calling like kids engaged in petty quarrels has created a backfire through the former US Ambassador to the Philippines Philip Goldberg who is also a victim of PDU30's not so "flowery words".

Like what I usually say in my daily radio program that the Duterte administration or anybody who has dealings with the US, they should be careful because speaking from experience, I know their ways and sentiments especially when it comes to character assassination so to speak.

From a source through the Manila Times, an article by Dr. Dante Ang - US ex-envoy plotting Duterte fall stated that source said former US Ambassador Philip Goldberg has outlined a list of "strategies" to undermine President Duterte and called for his eventual ouster. The blueprint gave a timetable of one-and-a-half years.

Quoting Goldberg, it said the "political actors (the opposition) would need all the political weapons in their arsenal to replace the Duterte administration and replace it with something more to the opposition's liking." He noted, however, "that (deposing Duterte) would be a challenge for the opposition."

Analyzing the President's weakness, Goldberg said that Mr. Duterte "has no real friends" outside of his region for his propensity to mock and ridicule people close to him. He also said that the President's "views are shaped not by ideology or personal ambitions, but by old-fashioned nationalism where he holds the United States accountable for the Philippines' current state of poverty and dependency."

To bring down Duterte, the alleged Goldberg plan calls for stoking public dissatisfaction with the President over unfulfilled election promises, isolating the Philippines from the rest of the ASEAN by extending military assistance to member countries except the Philippines, and/or through economic "blackmail" that aims to limit trade by some ASEAN member countries with the Philippines.

Goldberg also reportedly encourages support for the opposition through aids and grants, sowing discontent among the Duterte supporters and cultivating the cleavage between the congressmen and the senators over the Charter Change issue.

In brief, the plan calls on the US government to employ a combination of socio-economic-political-diplomatic moves against Duterte "to bring him to his knees and eventually remove him from office."

I did my part of reminding the President, time and again of the undercurrents that will translate to something else if not handled properly, locally and in the global front. The writings on the wall are very clear – signs of an impending storm in the offing.

The alleged predictions of former ambassador Goldberg will have a timetable of one-and-a-half years and the "strategies to be employed" are:

Political and economic isolation of the Philippines in the region by engaging the leaders of Japan, Vietnam, Cambodia and Laos and by "highlighting the basic question of the risk of doing business in the Philippines."

Enhanced US military relationship with members of the ASEAN community except the Philippines.

Blackmail neighboring countries so they would turn against Duterte by reducing trade with the Philippines in favor of Vietnam, Cambodia and Laos.

Deepen ties with Philippine officials (the opposition), the police/military and leaders in the region who share the US concerns over Duterte.

Track corruption cases and highlight the failures of Duterte.

"Focus on the needs of the people at the grassroots and assist the opposition groups in delivering those failed promises through USAID – such as alleviation of poverty, housing and education – to name a few."

Utilize the media to expose the truth about Duterte – "his false vision for the Filipino people and his dangerous international relationships with China and Russia."

Some might ask that exposing these alleged predictions of a former diplomat to the country is a warning and what will the new Trump administration will do, and in the process, who will benefit?

But the plot thickened when a close ally of PRRD, Mocha Uson who's now a columnist at Philippine Star exposed an ouster plot against the president and even fast tracking the plan. To quote, "There is also a rumor that some people are working to oust Duterte this 1st quarter of 2017. Are we just going to allow that to happen?"

Christmas in the Philippines is never postponed despite the unusual super typhoon but let us all be prepared for the coming storm in the coming new year.

Ooooo

DECEMBER 20, 2016
Prepare for the Worst

China appears to have installed weapons including anti-aircraft and anti-missile systems - on all seven of the artificial islands it has built in the South China Sea.

Last Wednesday, December 14, the Asia Maritime Transparency Initiative (AMTI), a US think-tank, said that its findings come despite statements by the Chinese leadership that Beijing has no intention of militarizing the islands in the strategic trade route, where territory is claimed by several countries.

AMTI said it has been tracking construction of hexagonal structures on Fiery Cross, Mischief, and Subi reefs in the Spratly Islands since June and July. China has already built military-length airstrips on these islands. "These gun and probable close-in weapons systems CIWS emplacements show that Beijing is serious about defense of its artificial islands in case of an armed contingency in the South China Sea," AMTI said. (Source: Reuters news agency)

And we thought (especially President Rody Duterte) that China has no intention of raising the already high tension in the contested area in the South China Sea but in reality China or shall we say President Xi Jinping did not stop or even hesitate in building the defense system to protect its interest in those reclaimed islands in the SCS.

We cannot blame the world's perception that China is actually pushing towards achieving its so called 'China dream' no matter what, even to the point of going to war and seeking an outside enemy in the process just to unite the Chinese nation.

If the independent foreign policy that PDU30 wants to implement means engaging friendship and cooperation with China and doing away with the international law principles and arguments based on UNCLOS, we are heading for trouble.

Engaging in bilateral talks with China is not as easy as a walk in the park in which PDU30 wants to adopt to settle the territorial disputes. As what former Assistant Secretary for ASEAN Affairs (1988-89) and Asian and Pacific Affairs (l997-1999) at the Department of Foreign Affairs, Juanito P. Jarasa writes in his article @manilatimes online – "As a member of the Philippine delegation to two high-level bilateral meetings with China regarding the South China Sea held in Beijing in May 1997 and Manila in March 1999, I saw how difficult it was to deal with China on a one-on-one basis. The Chinese wanted us to swallow hook, line, and sinker their "historic rights and indisputable sovereignty over the South China Sea" while rejecting international law principles and arguments based on UNCLOS. Unless China changes its mind about the Permanent Court of Arbitration ruling, I am afraid entering into bilateral negotiations with China will belike going into a cul-de-sac(dead end). Indications are strong that the South China Sea will remain as one of China's three core national interests, along with Taiwan and Tibet.

It seems the only hope for the Philippines, and the world for that matter, is for China to realize that the "China Dream" to bury its past humiliation in the hands of Western powers and to gain respect as a leading civilized state does not lie in disregard or disrespect of the rule of law but in abiding by the time-honored 'comitas gentium', or comity of nations. Merriam-Webster says that since 1862, comity of nations has referred to countries bound by a courteous relationship based on mutual recognition of executive, legislative, and judicial acts. In essence, comity entails friendship and respect among countries as well as mutual civility and courtesy between them. That could be hard to achieve in today's world beset by turmoil of various kinds but it is an ideal situation worth aspiring for."

But this China dream could be a tool to unite China and actually Xi Jinping's propaganda to save himself from so many angry Chinese which will soon realize that their losing their funds invested to the government.

Let us help this present administration realize that it is not easy to deal with China and put our country's security in danger. Let us pray for our president because no matter what, any wrong decision will drag us all down and face a war unwittingly in the process.

Who said that Digong's deal with the Marcoses is a jinx that will pull him down like anyone else who made deals with them? Just asking..

Ooooo

DECEMBER 13, 2016
Strategic Dilemma

If we thought that the tension in the contested area in the South China has already subsided due to some factors like change in leadership in some countries in the region, actually it didn't.

Based on the article of Peter Layton - The South China Sea's Worsening Strategic Dilemmas, he gave two possible scenarios, negative and positive that might occur in the SCS in the next seven years.

"Alternative futures represent a way for us to think about possible tomorrows. Imagine that the future lies somewhere between the best of all possible worlds and the worst, somewhere between a cooperative and a conflictual state. Neither extreme future is necessarily more likely than the other, but they allow us to think about the spectrum of possibilities. Using the cooperative and conflictual variables creates two possible alternative as follows:

The cooperative future will be considered by many to be wildly optimistic, while pessimistic realists will say that the conflictual world bears some resemblance to where we are now. But the task for policymakers is to steer the future towards the 'good' tomorrow and away from the 'bad' one. Worryingly, the two major strategic thrusts at the moment, driven by ASEAN and the United States, don't seem to be moving us in the good direction.

ASEAN is trying to encourage China to sign a Code of Conduct (COC), an agreement conceived as a binding preventive diplomacy measure that'll forestall conflict. Talks continue, as they have since 2002. Late 2017 is now the hope-for target date for completion of the code, or at least an agreed draft. China though has long argued—and formalized in various international agreements—that the South China Sea isn't a multilateral issue and so ASEAN as a grouping has no place discussing it. And in recent years China has convinced Cambodia, Laos and now the Philippines to embrace the PRC's South China Sea stance, making an ASEAN South China Sea consensus unlikely. More pointedly, why would China sign something that doesn't advance its interests?"

The year 2017 could be the deciding moment for President Rody Duterte as our country will be the host of the next ASEAN meeting. For obvious reason that PDU30 is now 'friendly' with China, and it seems a consensus among ASEAN members is farfetched to encourage China to sign the Code of Conduct, being the host country, our President must consider what the other members' stand on the COC in relation to the Code of Conduct. He must be sensitive enough not to hurt other ASEAN leaders because he favors China.

The mere fact that we purchased armaments from China, are we going to use them against our neighbors or from our long time ally? If the conflictual theory will prevail, like what I have been saying for quite some time now that if the program is on, yes it can be delayed but it will push through because the man made global crisis by the globalists whose interest is to depopulate the world, another world war is possible.

Our country will play a major role in this future war game for it to happen or not in Duterte's term, just like what president-elect Donald Trump said about not to meddle in other country's regime change, in the end the globalists will

Dr. Erick San Juan, D.Litt.   **80**

prevail and leaders will just be pawns in the chessboard of war mongers in the process.

Be wary!

Ooooo

DECEMBER 5, 2016
Fake News

We thought that the advancement in science and technology can weaponize vaccines and also manipulate weather to use it as weapon against target areas only, but there is another one that we never imagine that such evil geniuses will manipulate and use as weapon – the so called 'fake news' via the internet and mainstream media.

In his article "Is the US Government Behind the Fake News Media Attacks on President-elect Trump?" (12/4/16), Dr. Paul Craig Roberts writes - Eric Zuesse has brought to our attention that US intelligence officials have placed a story in Buzzfeed, "a Democratic party mouthpiece," that the Russian government used fake news to get Donald Trump elected president.

http://www.washingtonsblog.com/2016/12/63755.html

According to Buzzfeed:

US intelligence officials believe Russia helped disseminate fake and propagandized news as part of a broader effort to influence and undermine the presidential election, two US intelligence sources told BuzzFeed News.

'They're doing this continuously, that's a known fact,' one US intelligence official said, requesting anonymity to discuss the sensitive national security issue.

'This is beyond propaganda, that's my understanding,' the second US intelligence official said. The official said they believed those efforts likely included the dissemination of completely fake news stories. ...

One intelligence official said, 'In the context, did Russia attempt to influence the US elections; the aperture is as wide as it can possibly be.'" 'The real unanswered question is, why did they do it?, the second US intelligence official said. 'Is it because they love Donald Trump?

Because they hated Hillary Clinton? Or just because they like undermining Western democracies?'

Who are these US intelligence officials who are portraying the president-elect of the United States to be a "Putin stooge, a tool of Russia"?

Pundits advice that once in office, Trump must investigate these hostile elements in US intelligence who are working to discredit the US president and the American people who voted him into office.

As one reader pointed out, those who debunk "conspiracy theories," that is, explanations that they do not like, now have a conspiracy theory of their own: Vladimir Putin used independent American websites to elect Trump with fake news. Only voters living in a few large coastal cities were immune to the fake news.

In other words, the presstitute media has lost control over Americans' minds to Putin.

With an opponent, this powerful, neoconservatives better think a dozen times before fomenting any more tension with the Kremlin."

The use of weaponized fake news could actually lead to confrontation among nations and if such big nations are involved it might trigger a global conflict.

That is why the architects of these weaponized fake news had used all means to reach the masses day in and day out in all popular media outfits.

"You really know that masses of people are living within a mind-control matrix when the greatest, most pervasive purveyors of fake news denounce others for the practice." (Finian Cunningham)

Blaming others like alternative media and websites and credible blogsites is the scapegoat to lead the masses away from the truth and towards synthetic news.

Discussed with truth and credibility, Prof. Michel Chossudovsky in his article 'Who is Behind "Fake News"? Mainstream Media Use Fake Videos and Images' (Global Research, November 24, 2016) — "The mainstream corporate media is desperate.

They want to suppress independent and alternative online media, which it categorizes as "fake news".

Readers on social media are warned not to go onto certain sites.

The intent of this initiative is to smear honest reporting and Truth in Media.

Dr. Erick San Juan, D.Litt.

Our analysis confirms that some mainstream media are routinely involved in distorting the facts and turning realities upside down.

They are the unspoken architects of "Fake News".

One area of routine distortion is the use of fake videos and images by the mainstream media."

Prof. Chossudovsky has given Four Notorious Cases of Media Distortion and the most controversial and very deceiving was the news on 9/11.

Fake News regarding the Collapse of World Trade Center Building Seven in New York.

The most grotesque lie pertains to the BBC and CNN announcement in the afternoon of September 11, that WTC Building Seven (The Solomon Building) had collapsed.

The BBC report went live at 5.00pm, 21 minutes before the actual occurrence of the collapse, indelibly pointing to foreknowledge of the collapse of WTC 7.

CNN anchor Aaron Brown announced that the building "has either collapsed or is collapsing" about an hour before the event."

The regular users of Facebook has experienced one way or another as victims of fake news using images and videos that were altered. Finding only in the end that they were taken for a ride, maybe after they were corrected by friends or worst bullied and laughed at for the mistake believing it was for real.

Actually we have our own share of fake news, intended or not, or sometimes tagged as a joke, but it has created a controversy already so the people responsible for such boo-boo has to do a lot of explaining and corrections.

There will be court cases to be filed by major newspapers soon due to trolls and PR wrecking crew operators using newspaper letterheads in their psy war op.

So the famous line 'think before you click' or be careful in using all the facets in the internet so as not to create trouble, should be in the minds of all users. Be wise and avoid being the carrier of fake news.

Ooooo

NOVEMBER 30, 2016
TPP: Calculated Risk

If we have our own 'change is coming' ala Duterte style, with President elect Donald Trump of the world's superpower, changes are coming too and one of these changes is the withdrawal of the US from the Trans-Pacific Partnership Program or TPP.

US President Barack Obama is the one who pushed for the TPP together with his pivot to Asia back in 2011.

The Obama administration and many in the business community view the deal as both an economic opportunity and in some ways a foreign policy one.

In terms of foreign policy, Obama and his team saw the deal as part of a broader strategy to assert American values and interests both in Asia and around the world in opposition to China's growing power and influence.

China is not included in the TPP. Instead, the deal comprises a diverse group of nations (Australia, Brunei, Canada, Chile, Japan, Malaysia, Mexico, New Zealand, Peru, Singapore and Vietnam) that the U.S. wanted to build stronger economic ties with.

Obama argued that by helping write the trade agreement that set policy for a wide group of nations, the United States could push for higher labor and environmental standards abroad. This would benefit American workers, he argued, because it would mean that companies in the TPP nations would abide by workplace standards that more closely resembled those in the U.S. With more equitable workplace standards, there would be fewer incentives for American companies to treat their workers poorly or outsource their jobs abroad.

The administration argued that the more direct benefit for Americans would be expanded and simplified trade with many of these nations. Obama's team estimated the TPP would lift 18,000 tariffs imposed on U.S. products sold abroad. This would lower the price of American-made products abroad and therefore potentially increase their sales, which could create jobs back home.

Obama did not state this so bluntly, but his argument is essentially that the trends that are causing

American jobs to disappear — more international trade, technology, globalization, and automation — are not going away, and trade agreements like TPP can help the U.S. thrive in the new economy.

But soon-to-be US President Trump has different views on the TPP.

With the TPP, 12 countries would have been able to share in the perks of this free trade bonanza. That involves the reduction or elimination of tariffs (a tax or duty to be paid on goods), new rules for resolving trade disputes, and the renegotiation of subsidies for the manufacturing and agricultural sectors, among many, many other very complicated things.

Trump's beef with the TPP is that he claims it will hurt American workers and undercut US companies. His stance on trade is protectionist: he believes that the average American farmer and auto worker has lost out from the fact that labor is cheap in developing countries like China, Vietnam, and Malaysia.

He's definitely not wrong here—many low-skilled jobs that used to belong to the backbone of American industrial towns have been shipped overseas because, hey, if no one (read: the government) is stopping profit-driven corporations from lowering production costs, what incentive would they have to continue manufacturing products in higher cost jurisdictions like the US?

"Instead of negotiating with 12 countries in the TPP, he thinks he can get a better deal for Americans if there are fewer countries at the table," says Stuart Trew, trade economist at the Canadian Centre for Policy Alternatives and co-author of "The Trans-Pacific Partnership & Canada: A Citizen's Guide." "These are interesting times for trade. Trump is shaking up the orthodoxy."

Indeed, the TPP has long been touted by critics as a grand American plan to plant their flag in East Asia and counter the perceived economic threat that is China, by getting first dibs in trade negotiations with key growth markets in Asia-Pacific like Australia, Brunei, Vietnam, and Malaysia.

But with the pledge of president elect Donald Trump, to dump or to renegotiate the TPP, a window of opportunity is now open to China.

China is now positioning itself as free trade's new champion and seizing economic leadership of the Pacific Rim.

Under President Barack Obama the TPP was sold as a way to counter China's rise, and its possible demise is now viewed in China as a US retreat from the region.

Chinese President Xi Jinping has seized the opportunity at the APEC summit last weekend and pushed his own free trade vision, the Regional Comprehensive Economic Partnership (RCEP).

It involves 16 countries including Australia and Japan, but excludes America.

Mr. Xi is pushing to make it bigger and is leaving the door open to Latin American countries like Peru who are keen to benefit from the growing economies of Asia.

The move would be a massive boost for China's plans to shift the existing US-dominated world economic order.

With billions of dollars on offer, China is trying to supplant the World Bank and the IMF with its Asia Infrastructure Investment Bank.

Now that China is picking off ASEAN countries one by one through the Regional Comprehensive Economic Partnership (RCEP), will China rise as the new economic power using its cash diplomacy?

Malaysian Prime Minister Najib Razak signed off on US$34 billion ($46 billion) in trade and investment agreements.

A couple of weeks earlier, Philippines President Rodrigo Duterte signed US$13 billion ($17 billion) in trade and aid deals.

Cambodia was already on side but to secure support Beijing offered 31 trade agreements and US$300 million ($406 million). Now attention is turning to Thailand, which since its military coup in 2014 is tilting towards China.

One by one China is picking off the ASEAN countries that were traditionally aligned to America and united against China's territorial claims in the South China Sea.

China's control in the South China Sea is as much about economics as it is national pride. About US$5 trillion ($6.7 trillion) — or half the world's trade — moves through the waters of the South China Sea.

Controlling and regulating those waterways will give China enormous power in setting the economic rules of the game.

To achieve this China is breaking the template that has been in place since the end of Word War II — most Asian nations accepted American security guarantees and were then left to focus on economic growth, stability and prosperity.

In the new Chinese order the remaining ASEAN countries face a choice. If they want to benefit from China's chequebook diplomacy then the cost might be to accept China's claims over the South China Sea.

At the end of the day China hopes to cleave ASEAN from America's grasp and make the United States strategic pivot back into Asia unworkable.

They are counting on Donald Trump as president advocating a more isolationist stance.

Although Trump's administration will begin in January 2017, the present confluence of events might lead to global financial crisis beginning with the US Federal Reserve possible rate increase and the outcome could be devastating to at least four big national banks including the European Union and China.

And if this means trouble, is the inevitable global war still in the offing? And as a nation, are we prepared?

Research Sources:

Here's why Trump hates the Trans-Pacific Partnership so much By Vanmala Subramaniam, VICE News Nov. 25, 2016

Trump's Pledge to Dump the TPP Just First Step in Anti-Trade Agenda by Perry Bacon Jr. (NBC News) November 23, 2016

Trans-Pacific Partnership: China seizes trade opportunity after Donald Trump's threat - Analysis By China correspondent Matthew Carney (ABC News) November 24, 2016

Ooooo

NOVEMBER 22, 2016
Never Learned from History

It seems that after over six months, the election fever is still on and the country's socio-political gap is getting wider as crucial issues emerged. The latest of which is the 'surprise burial' of the former President Ferdinand E. Marcos at the Libingan ng mga Bayani last November 18 at 12 high noon.

It will be remembered that Marcos' burial is in the election promise list during the campaign period of team DU30 and allegedly in return for the campaign donation given by the Marcoses. It was even confirmed by President Rody Duterte in one of his interviews that Ilocos Norte Gov. Imee Marcos donated for his campaign funds.

So the big fuss that the anti-Marcos/anti-Martial Law protesters are staging is due to the fact that the burial was likened to a thief in the night and a lot were surprised. Former President Ramos got pissed off that despite his meeting with PRRD last week, he was not informed not even by his boys who are now in the cabinet of DU30.

Duterte has defended the burial, saying laws entitled Marcos to be buried at the heroes' cemetery as a former president and soldier. Although varied reports said that PDU30 was not aware of the Marcos burial last November 18 and the flowers from Malacanang was a SOP (standard procedure).

Is PDU30 convinced by the Marcoses to fast track all legal remedies so that the FM secret accounts in the Carribean under a shell corporation at the British Virgin Islands be recovered before the globalists garnished it due to the expose of the Panama Papers?

Aside from the so-called Martial Law victims and protesters, former President Fidel Ramos, once again reminded President Duterte to be very careful of his decisions that concerns almost healed wounds from the past.

The number one supporter and a staunch believer of a Duterte presidency, PFVR said that the move of the Marcos family to hasten the burial of the patriarch, with the help of the police and military, is a "step backwards" for the Duterte administration.

"You must understand that is just a happening in a series of happenings. The scheme of the Marcos family with the connivance of some elements of Armed Forces including the national police -- some only, not everybody -- is a step backwards for this administration in the sense that they are losing support, they are losing friends," Ramos said. (Various sources)

Is the former president's statement a warning to the present administration to be cautious of things to come that may contribute to his downfall if he will not heed the writings on the wall? Just asking.

The alleged payback of the Marcos donation through the burial of the 'dictator' at the LNMB can be a trigger to a series of events that might be a repeat of the Erap ouster in 2001. Duterte should make decisions based on intelligent advises from people who know more like PFVR on matters of politics, diplomacy and national security.

Now that the outrage of the netizens and the millenials from the internet (via social media networking) to the streets is gaining momentum, are we geared towards a social volcano in the offing ready to erupt any moment now?

No matter how often people say to move on when it comes to the Marcos' burial, it is quite obvious why the past administrations did not touch such controversial issue because wounds of hate and anger will pry open and create a divided nation in the process. Everything will be affected, people will turn to parliament of the streets and economic activities will be hampered. And here we go again, just like in the 70's when Martial Law was declared, same old chants and placards, and same old, now old activists and protesters of the Marcos years.

Some say that this 'Marcos' political victory' is a step closer for the younger Marcos, Jr. to win the second highest position of the land. What? We have been fooled once, and maybe twice but another Marcos in the Palace? WTF! Never again!

Let us not allow another deception by the family that plundered this nation and when exiled, helped by people like me and the original Marcos loyalists hoping that they will acknowledge and grant what was promised and be given what due us. Nothing. Many of the original loyalists got sick and died without even visited, assisted nor given condolences by any one of the family despite that they're all back and in government service. The worst, my good friend, Col. Rexor Ver, one of the sons of the late Fabian Ver died without getting any assistance for his medication from this family. All but empty promises and lies.

Let us all learn from history and never to allow a repeat.

Ooooo

NOVEMBER 16, 2016
Is Marxism Dead?

Pray that the Obama/ Clinton/global elitist cabal hasn't found the Marxist way to compromise the promise of Tuesday night, because it's still a long way between now and January 20, 2017 Inauguration. (Source: Marxists still looking for the way to compromise Tuesday's election by Judi McLeod)

Will there be a coup even before the president-elect takes its oath of office as the new US President?

In the article by Doug Hagmann last November 12 he writes, it is now Hillary Clinton and her Marxist supporters who are threatening our Representative Republic through the petition website Change.org. Immediately following Donald Trump's election victory, a petition was launched to sway the Electoral College to "Make Hillary Clinton President on December 19.

The Electoral College will meet and vote on December 19, 2016, to certify the Trump victory as defined within our Constitution. Remember, the United States is a Representative Republic and not a Democracy, no matter how many times journalists want to change our constitution through language and the repetitiveness of their lies.

It is typical for the Clintons and those in their camp to do the exact opposite of what they say publicly. This has been proven through the Wikileaks release of Hillary Clinton's speeches to big money interests behind closed doors confirming that what she says and does in public is not consistent with what she says to (and does for) her private, big dollar supporters and special interest groups.

Unable to comprehend such duplicity and blinded by their idolatry, these useful idiots, including the Hollywood elite are pushing for the Electors of the Electoral College to cast their ballots for Clinton on December 19, 2016. They believe that they have the chance to change the outcome of the election, an event that would surely throw this already heavily divided country into a very real civil war, something the Marxists Progressives have been longing for. Sounds familiar! In fact, my own government insider admitted as much exactly as I have documented in my previous reports.

As to the petition to the Electoral College, it should be noted that they currently have over 2.2 million "signatures" and are gaining on their goal of three million. No one should think that the globalist power structure, for which Hillary Rodham Clinton is the face, will willingly cede their power. They will not go quietly into the night. Unless a secret concession will be ok'd by incoming President Trump as told. Instead, they will utilize the tactics of their patron saint, Saul Alinsky, whose book Rules for Radicals was dedicated to Lucifer himself. We are seeing this play out on the streets of Portland, Los Angeles, New York and other cities in between."

If we have liberation theologists and Maoists support thru the National Democratic Front, Communist Party of the Philippines and New People's Army, in America its the secret funds of China through pro-Beijing big business Chinese based in the US funding the Marxists. We have to remember that the same Chinese block supported the presidency of Bill Clinton. So its a no-no this time from the Zionists who really control America. I was even shock to know that some agit-props in the US are NDF US base supporting Hillary.

I'm right after all that's the main reason why the super elites shifted their secret support to Trump.

But is Donald Trump really an anti-establishment president?

"The establishment is concerned that Trump would "shake-up" long standing policies under the Democratic and Republican duopoly that benefited private interest groups:

He promised to build a wall along the Mexican border and temporarily bar Muslim immigrants from entering the United States. He questioned Washington's longstanding commitment to NATO allies, called for cutting foreign aid, praised President Vladimir V. Putin of Russia, vowed to rip up international trade deals, assailed China and suggested Asian allies develop nuclear weapons.

"I will build a great, great wall on our southern border. And I will have Mexico pay for that wall" Trump said in 2015. Trump's plan to build a wall along the borders of Mexico will not stop immigrants from crossing the borders without addressing the North American Free Trade Agreement (NAFTA) which has devastated millions of small Mexican farmers.

As for NATO troops who are supported by U.S. taxpayers, Trump told Charles Lane and the editorial board of the Washington Post on March 21st, that he does "not" want to pull out NATO. Here is what he said: No, I don't want to pull it out. NATO was set up at a different time. NATO was set up when we were a richer country. We're not a rich country. We're borrowing, we're borrowing all of this money. We're borrowing money from China, which is a sort of an amazing situation. But things are a much different thing. NATO is costing us a fortune and yes, we're protecting Europe but we're spending a lot of money. Number 1, I think the distribution of costs has to be changed. I think NATO as a concept is good, but it is not as good as it was when it first evolved. And I think we bear the, you know, not only financially, we bear the biggest brunt of it. Obama has been stronger on the Ukraine than all the other countries put together, and those other countries right next door to the Ukraine. And I just say we have, I'm not even knocking it, I'm just saying I don't think it's fair, we're not treated fair. I don't think we're treated fair, Charles, anywhere. If you look everything we have. You know, South Korea is very rich. Great industrial country. And yet we're not reimbursed fairly for what we do. We're constantly, you know, sending our ships, sending our planes, doing our war games, doing other. We're reimbursed a fraction of what this is all costing. Trump will support NATO as long as the EU pays for it.

One other positive note, Trump does want a better relationship with Russia who has been fighting alongside Syrian government forces against the Islamic State. Trump wants the U.S. and Russian forces to work together to defeat the Islamic State. Putin has expressed his willingness to work with Trump to rebuild a relationship that is mutually beneficial. The New York Times also made accusations that "with Mr. Trump praising Mr. Putin and

American investigators concluding that Russians had hacked Democratic email messages." There is no proof that Russia hacked the Democratic National Convention's (DNC) emails or that Trump is linked to Vladimir Putin." (Source: Is it Fact or Fiction? US Media Says that New World Order is in Jeopardy with a Trump Presidency by Timothy Alexander Guzman, Global Research, November 11, 2016)

But what concerns most of us on the other side of the globe, the biggest continent, Asia, What Does Trump Victory Mean for Asia? An "Isolationist America" or More "Soft Power"? as what was cited by The New Atlas @globalresearch.ca last November 10 – "With the victory of Donald Trump during the 2016 US presidential elections, many commentators, analysts and academics have "predicted" a more isolationist America. For Asia specifically, particularly those in need of US intervention to prop up their unpopular, impotent political causes, they fear an ebbing of US support.

However, as history has shown, the whims of US voters rarely has an impact on US foreign policy, particularly amidst the more subtle use of US "soft power."

US policy toward Asia has been a historical, socioeconomic and military continuum marked by a consistent desire for geopolitical and socioeconomic primacy in the region stretching back for over a century. Since World War 2, the US has attempted to contain a rising China, temper and exploit emerging developing nations across Southeast Asia and prevent nations subjugated to US domination (Japan, South Korea and the Philippines) from achieving anything resembling an independent foreign and domestic policy.

This is a continuum that has transcended presidential administrations and congressional shifts of power for decades.

The networks that primarily seek to establish, protect and expand US primacy in Asia are driven by corporate and financial special interests including banks, the energy industry, defense contractors, agricultural and pharmaceutical giants, the US entertainment industry and media as well as tech giants.

They achieve primacy through a variety of activities ranging from market domination through incremental advances in "free trade," the funding of academic and activist groups through organizations like the US National Endowment for Democracy (NED), Open Society, Freedom House and USAID as well as direct pressure on the governments of respective Asian states through both overt and covert political, economic and military means.

This is a process that takes place independent of both the White House and the US Congress.

Regardless of how elections turn out, this process will continue so long as the source of these collective special interests' power remains intact and unopposed.

For Asian states, in the wake of Trump's victory, keeping track of and dealing with the actual networks used to project American primacy into Asia Pacific is more important than weighing the isolationist rhetoric of president-elect Donald Trump."

There are a lot to speculate on a Trump administration, like our own president, surprises and maybe blunders will surely occur for days to come.

Just like what President Obama said today to Trump, "Trump soon to face sobering reality check". Meaning- who's the real boss? Who rules?

Ooooo

NOVEMBER 9, 2016
Yolanda Debacle

The commemoration of the 3rd anniversary of the super typhoon Yolanda's devastation in the Visayas was once again marred with the shortcomings of the previous administration. Funds were allegedly missing because the victims of the calamity are still suffering from poor living conditions.

Organizations under the auspices of the United Nations kept saying that our country is one of the vulnerable nations that has and will greatly suffer due to climate change. May it be dry or wet season, we experienced a great loss of lives and properties because of the so-called climate change (a.k.a. global warming).

Actually this could be the reason why the former president Fidel Ramos got pissed off when President Rody Duterte reiterated his stand against the signing of the Paris

Agreement on Climate Change. It was in July that PDU30 hinted in his speech that he will not honor the climate change pact on carbon emission.

But last November 7, during a speech at the oath-taking of the new officers of the National Press Club in Malacañang Palace, the president announced his decision that he will now back the Paris Agreement on Climate Change, after a near-unanimous approval by his Cabinet, and he will be signing the historic pact.

According to the 2016 Climate Change Vulnerability Index, the Philippines is one of the 15 countries most vulnerable to climate change. But what is the Paris Agreement all about?

According to the article of Tony La Viña (former dean of the Ateneo School of Government) @rappler.com, "The Paris Agreement is not just a carbon emissions agreement but a comprehensive sustainable development agreement. It is an adaptation, loss and damage, finance, technology and capacity building agreement – all of which are essential to our survival. We cannot cherry-pick but have to accept the whole package. But we can do so in our own terms.

To opt out of the Paris Agreement is to allow developed countries to escape from their responsibility to compensate us for causing climate change. The Paris Agreement is the only process where we can get developed countries to be accountable for their emissions through a loss and damage mechanism and through provisions that require them as a matter of climate justice to provide support to us so we can adapt to and mitigate climate change. Indeed, the Paris Agreement has good provisions on finance, technology transfer, and capacity building. Our delegation worked hard in Paris to get the best text possible for these provisions.

The Paris Agreement does not impose emissions reduction limitations on us. We can determine our own targets based on our development needs. We can adopt targets but we can make that conditional on support by developed countries. That's what we did in Paris – we did offer 70% but we said we will do it only if support was given. If the Duterte administration wishes, it can lower the number to maybe 30-40% and perhaps commit to do 10-15% of that as unconditional since we are already doing many things on our own. Such a decision would be credible and acceptable.

The Paris Agreement is a good document whose consequences will last generations. While this legally binding agreement in itself is not enough to solve the climate crisis, it is as strong, ambitious, and as equitable as it can be for an agreement that required consensus by 195 countries—a positive beginning to a long and hard journey towards climate justice."

Yes, there are concerted efforts of countries around the world to address the so called threats of global warming/climate change but as what we have been saying for several years now in our radio program and in our writings that there is one element that this body is missing or has refused to acknowledge, which is the man-made cause of climate change, that is weather manipulation or weather engineering.

Strange behavior of weather systems and abnormal movements of typhoons that we have never before witnessed are the signatures of someone or something is really manipulating Mother Nature that has caused great dangers to humankind.

Could it be that through this evil science of manipulating weather is the reason for people of various nations to be compelled to sign a pact to address the man made disaster? In the various UN-sponsored gatherings of leaders of various nations, there is always opposition to such move because it will only hamper the growth and development of countries especially the developing ones.

Treaties that will only manipulate nations and like a herd of cattle, will lead them to the slaughterhouse because the real culprit of such world disaster such as global warming is actually known as man-made and it will go on as long as the evil geniuses behind it are not exposed and punish.

Who may taught that such weather engineering is only seen in the sci-fi movies?

Ooooo

NOVEMBER 1, 2016
Is The Honeymoon Period Over?

The first 100 days of the Duterte administration has shown several good and bad aspects in its governance. Those who voted for DU30 gradually find mistakes and a lot of blunders especially in his style of using cuss words. Campaign supporters suddenly turned sour and now become critics to the administration's shortcomings. Is the honeymoon period over? What went wrong? Is there an exodus of supporters turning sour already?

The number one supporter and the man who believed he can do it as the president of the land is no other than former president Fidel Ramos. Now a supporter-turned-critic, PFVR wrote in his articles what a true leader is and how he sees the Filipinos being led in the wrong direction. Even pundits accepted DU30 as a 'necessary evil' in a divided nation. But oppositors believed that former President Ramos created a 'Frankenstein' out of Digong. Of course the diehard Duterte fans in turn criticize PFVR, and in the long run we are again divided. Is this what we hoped for and asked for after being led to the pits of the previous administration's 'tuwid na daan'? Where are the promised changes?

Ramos said from day one, a national leader must define where he will bring the nation and show the people how to get there. He leads by setting the right example that the citizenry should emulate. He leads by making the correct decisions for the betterment of the many, not the enrichment of the few.

The bottom line is, Ramos said, Duterte cannot do it alone. Nether can the government do it alone.

"But when all of us strive together with one goal in mind, and abide by the same precious values and commitments—we become a strong nation, able to achieve the higher quality of life we have always yearned for—in an environment of enduring peace and sustainable development," he said.

He added that the government was "losing badly" after Duterte's first 100 days because the administration gave priority to the war on drugs at the expense of

Dr. Erick San Juan, D.Litt.   **97**

alleviating poverty, bringing down the cost of living, attracting foreign investments and generating jobs. (Source: PH a sinking ship — FVR by Sandy Araneta @manilastandard)

PFVR was right because of the so much attention given to the war on drugs and criminality, but where are the big fishes? Why eliminate the poor people who are victims of hardships and unemployment? The war on poverty was not addressed and it was shown on the latest survey that the government should now focus on the poverty issue and generating jobs. The common (tao) people most probably DU30's supporters are now asking the present leadership to put the war on drugs operation in the back burner and have real and tangible government policies that will help the poor Pinoys in their day-to-day struggle to survive.

Another very crucial matter that is being overlooked by the DU30's administration due to his war on drugs is the country's security from external threats. For the president, the war on drugs is too big that the national police is not enough and so he also included the armed forces to help in the campaign against drug users, dealers and protectors. Added to this is his campaign to bring an end to the Abu Sayyaf menace in the south that has sent several troops in the area instead of getting the mastermind and financier who basically owns the businesses in Sulu and nearby provinces to lessen the collateral damage and deaths of our soldiers.

Now the crucial question lies in the external and maritime defense that we needed badly in this exciting time where the rumblings of a possible world war is in the offing. External threat is always there especially Duterte announced the suspension of maritime patrol with the US on the country's coastal area.

With the endless verbal attack on the US, the United Nations and the EU, with the possible termination of agreements and ties with them, are we headed to deliberately weakening our capabilities and defense in relation to our alliances in case a war broke out.

The present leadership is perceived dragging the whole country to the wrong direction when it comes to foreign policy and diplomacy among nations. The growing number of Filipinos who are in favor of the US than China is already a clear sign that we must not trust China wholeheartedly and do away with Washington's help in the process.

We are approaching a year of global turbulence and a helping hand from an old ally will somehow help us get through during the hard times. Unless President DU30 changes his mind on certain important matters such as this, we will all go down with him unwittingly,

God forbid!

Ooooo

OCTOBER 25, 2016
"Galit sa Mundo"

"[The damage control] is the latest in a string of flip-flops, walk-backs and backtracks that have come to define Duterte's tenure, leaving Filipino and foreign observers unsure where rhetoric ends and real policy moves begin."
— The Washington Post, October 21

The above-mentioned excerpt from The Washington Post is just one of the many published reactions from international news organizations that had put our country in the limelight again due to the careless not-so-thought about comments from President Rody Duterte.

Such play of words also created a divided Philippines, those who are for and against the current administration, and recently after the China trip, those who are for and against China and the US.

Since the campaign period people in the Duterte's loop were saying that it is his style of speaking with several use of bad words and name-calling against people. Maybe the DU30 is still in the transition period from being just a mayor of a provincial city to the highest position of the land. He forgot to leave in Davao City his attitude where he can say bad words and be very brutally frank to people without having second thoughts. Of course the effect of such manners, now that he is the president is very different, not just national but worldwide.

He had to internalize the importance of being the leader of a nation and act like one. Being brave and patriotic for the good of one's country are not the issues, it is how he treats leaders of other countries or organizations. DU30's ways can be classified as somehow barbaric, we are now living in a world of civilized people and more so living interdependently among nations.

People in his loop will not always kowtow to his whims and will not do the backtracking and apologizing for him especially when the situation can really be very complicated that might lead to international sanctions among others.

Various experts have expressed their views on the latest flip-flop of DU30 while in Beijing. Like a true expert in their field of geopolitics and diplomacy, the line of DU30 on the independent foreign policy issue vis-à-vis our US military and economic ties are worth considering so as to avoid unexpected confluence of events.

One such analysis about independent foreign policy came from Francisco Tatad:

"I do not at all wonder, and no one else should, why President Duterte has been talking of an "independent foreign policy." What puzzles me, as it should everybody else, is why neither he nor his foreign secretary, Perfecto Yasay Jr., has said how the government intends to carry it out. By asking the US forces in Mindanao to leave? By dismantling the Enhanced Defense Cooperation Agreement with the US? By buying weapons from China and Russia? Every Tom, Dick and Harry wants to throw in his two cents' worth.

Section 7 of Article II—Declaration of Principles and State Policies—-is clear: "The State shall pursue an independent foreign policy. In relations with other states the paramount consideration shall be national sovereignty, territorial integrity, national interest, and the right to self-determination." Each of the four phrases is known, if vaguely, to the average citizen. Otherwise the Constitution and the spirit of our laws make them plain.

"The Philippines is a democratic and republican state," says the first section of Article II. "Sovereignty resides in the people and all government authority emanates from them."

National territory is that over which we exercise jurisdiction and control, and whose borders no state should try to change or promote secessionism within.

National interest, or "raison d'Etat" (reason of State) to the French, has a long history that evolved from the 1648 Peace of Westphalia that ended the Thirty Years War. We know it as our own political, economic, military and cultural goals and ambitions as distinguished from those of our closest friends and allies.

DU30 has proclaimed his desire to pursue an "independent foreign policy," but has yet to pronounce what he means. Does "independent" mean renouncing any security alliance with our current major ally? If so, this would mean scrapping the Mutual Defense Treaty with the US, the Visiting Forces Agreement and the Enhanced Defense Cooperation Agreement, and possibly pursuing a policy of neutrality like the Vatican or Switzerland."

The mere fact that we are historically part of every existing international groupings with specific missions and objectives to live harmoniously, in just one utterance from a city mayor-turned-president all these will be a thing of the past? Duh? Diplomacy and interdependence are not as simple as that.

Rhetoric is rhetoric. National foreign policy is different, it should be planned and discussed among experts in and out of the government. DU30 must consult experts in proper diplomacy, how it works and why it is needed in international protocols.

Many pundits are worried and asking why the president is acting with mixed emotion? "Parang galit sa mundo." Meaning him against the world. Cussing and calling world leaders who irritates him names. It is believed that these leaders and allies might not ignore his antics and will not take those insults sitting down which could drag us into chaos. Remember what happened to the late Indonesian President Sukarno. I hope it will not happen here.

Lastly, if he really loves this nation and the Filipino people, he should have raised the South China Sea issue with China and now with Japan, the issue of the Filipino comfort women. Need we say more?

Ooooo

OCTOBER 18, 2016
Threats

"Why is US President Barack Obama threatening Russia with World War 3 right before the election?" A very profound question and actually the title of the article by Michael Snyder published at redflagnews.com which he began with "It sure seems like an odd time to be provoking a war with Russia. As I write this, we stand just a little bit more than three weeks away from one of the most pivotal elections in U.S. history, and Barack Obama has chosen this moment to strongly threaten the Russians. Reuters reported that Obama is contemplating "direct U.S. military action" against Syrian military targets, and the Russians have already indicated that any assault on Syrian forces would be considered an attack on themselves. The rapidly deteriorating crisis in Syria has already caused tensions with Russia to rise to the highest level since the end of the Cold War."

Maybe a lot will wonder why Russia and the United States are dragged into this civil war inside Syria. Here is the analysis of Michael Snyder : "But without a doubt the crisis in Syria is not going to be resolved any time soon because it is one giant mess. Most people don't realize that the Syrian civil war has essentially been a proxy war between Sunni Islam and Shia Islam from the very beginning. Jihadist rebels that are being armed and funded by Saudi Arabia and Turkey are fighting Hezbollah troops that are being armed and funded by Iran. And now Turkish forces have invaded northern Syria, and this threatens to cause a full-blown war to erupt between Turkey and the Syrian Kurds. Of course ISIS is right in the middle of everything causing havoc, blowing stuff up and beheading anyone that doesn't believe in their radical version of Sunni Islam.

It is absolutely insane that the United States and Russia could potentially go to war because of this conflict. Both sides are determined to show the other how tough they are, and one false move could set off a spiral of events from which there may be no recovery."

Just like a ticking bomb, any false move or maybe a false flag operation orchestrated by covert operatives, the world can be dragged to another world war.

In the heat of the November US elections, barely three weeks to go, the Obama administration accused Russia of hacking and meddling with the coming election.

"The Obama administration is contemplating an unprecedented cyber covert action against Russia in retaliation for alleged Russian interference in the American presidential election, U.S. intelligence officials told NBC News.

Current and former officials with direct knowledge of the situation say the CIA has been asked to deliver options to the White House for a wide-ranging "clandestine" cyber operation designed to harass and 'embarrass' the Kremlin leadership.

The sources did not elaborate on the exact measures the CIA was considering, but said the agency has already begun opening cyber doors, selecting targets and making other preparations for an operation.

Somebody should tell Obama that he is not playing a video game. A cyber attack is considered to be an act of war, and the Russians would inevitably retaliate. And considering how exceedingly vulnerable our cyber infrastructure is, I don't know if that is something that we want to invite.

At the end of last week, Vice President Joe Biden also publicly threatened the Russians...

On Friday, Vice President Joe Biden met "Meet the Press" host Chuck Todd for an interview that has raised serious concern in Russia.

Without bothering to question the authenticity of the claims, Todd took the allegations of Russian hacking at face value, opening his interview with a loaded question: "Why haven't we sent a message yet to Putin?"

After a moment of stunned silence, Biden responded, "We're sending a message. We have the capacity to do it and it will be at the time of our choosing, and under the circumstances that will have the greatest impact."

When Todd asked if the public will know a message was sent, Biden replied, "Hope not."

The Russians firmly deny that they have any involvement in the hacking, and so far the Obama administration has not publicly produced any firm evidence that the Russians were behind it.

Perhaps the Obama administration privately has some evidence, but at this point they have not shown that evidence to the American public." (Ibid)

From a possible shooting war to cyber war, either way there seems to be no stopping this madness unless cooler heads will interfere and prevail. Until then the Russians are being advised through their state-owned television channel that they have to be prepared for a possible US nuclear attack and always be alert as to where they can find the nearest bomb shelter, just in case.

Are these threats and wars the necessary evil to achieve a one world control? Is Obama being programmed to do an FDR (Pres. Franklin Delano Roosevelt) war presidency which could hijack the November US presidential elections?

The big powers are actually preparing for the big one, a nuclear war, how about us? Still trapped with politics and a lot of word wars and rhetoric. When are we going to gather our act together and prepare for the worst?

Ooooo

OCTOBER 11, 2016
Elder's Advice

'Colorful person' and a person with 'colorful language' that is President Rody Duterte according to US President Barack Obama and Jose Almonte (former national security adviser). The former attribute may refer to a politician who can be seen dealing across the political spectrum, from left to right. While the latter, a description given to Pres. Duterte or shall I say a criticism, due to his use of cuss words especially to foreign top officials and organizations.

A hundred days of the 6-year term of the Duterte administration has been colorful enough that almost everyday in the tri-media, here and abroad, he always have those quotable quotes – may be good or bad to fill in that has caused the trending and debates between the for and against the president.

Even the former president and statesman in the international community as the most traveled leader of the country, former Pres. Fidel V. Ramos gave his comments on the performance of Pres. Duterte on his first 100 days in office. For him, Team Philippines is losing due to some incidents and broken promises. For PFVR, the status of the Philippines in the world as a community is important especially our economic and military ties with the United States.

Our status as an ally of the US with several existing treaties, from economic to military had gone a long, long way that will just end because Pres. Rody says so.

Like what PFVR said in his column, "are we throwing away decades of military partnership, tactical proficiency, compatible weaponry, predictable logistics, and soldier-to-soldier camaraderie just like that?

FVR's focus regarding this assessment of Du30's first 100 days is based simply on two concepts of primordial importance – LEADERSHIP and TEAMWORK – because that is where the perceived failures have emerged at this point in time.

Let all do-gooders, Pres. Rody included, please help the president's trusted lieutenants Jun Yasay(DFA), Lorenzana (DND), Ernie Abella and others clarify, contextualize, disbewilder, soothe, detoxify and otherwise enlighten most of us who believe that -in the 21st century – harmony, peace, inclusiveness, connectivity, and mutual benefit, etc. are people's highest aspirations."

As for Ms. Carmen N. Pedrosa in her column – 'Joal's reluctant admiration of Duterte', she writes – "Both he (Jo Almonte) and President Duterte come from lower middle class (not rich but not very poor either). It is from these origins that both strove to make something of themselves through self-study and use real life experiences as their higher education.

They have developed extraordinary careers in their chosen fields of endeavor. Joal as an intellectual soldier (hard to find these days) and Duterte as an unorthodox politician (a rara avis). On the unorthodox politician most of us thought it would take a miracle to have one and win as President in an elite-dominated society like the Philippines. You must be acceptable to big business.

Almonte conceded that Duterte has done well, fulfilling most of his campaign promises in his first 100 days.

He admitted it was Duterte's approach to the country's fundamental problems – "internal war, broken politics and monopolized business." He said Duterte's record was exceptional. But like many others he criticized the President for his "colorful language."

I beg to differ.

I think it was this "colorful language" that connected him with the masses and that to me is the most significant job in putting this country together. It is divided not just by politics as we know it. "Let us all be friends" is not the mantra for a well-run democratic society. What is, is "how to manage our differences" with strong institutions.

I don't know how Duterte developed his "colorful language." Did he plan it or did it come to him naturally that it was the style needed to get the attention and friendship of the masses?

I think Almonte referring to Duterte's "colorful language" was more concerned with his tirades against President Obama and other western leaders. It is obviously coming from a deeply felt anti-colonialism.

Almonte says he (PRRD) should tone down his language. It detracts from his accomplishments.

I do not think so. Netanyahu also told Obama to go to hell but got what he wanted anyway. US criticisms of his war on illegal drugs, Duterte also told Obama to "go to hell" and warned he may decide to "break up with America." There are other examples but it is not true that polite language is more effective. Rightly or wrongly polite language represents the power of the status quo when they ask Duterte to conform.

Duterte wants to change the world order into something less hypocritical. The history of US-Philippine relations shows that the "good boy" behavior only gets them bullied.

But Duterte has a wild card – a review of the (EDCA) Enhanced Defense Cooperation Agreement which President Obama carried home with speed and haste before we even realized how it would affect our security and well-being.

President Duterte has said it often enough that his foreign policy is to be friends with everyone, including the United States and China. But to put such foreign policy in place, he must give notice to the world that it will no longer be America's patsy in the region.

Dr. Erick San Juan, D.Litt.   **106**

Joal must have had a tough time maneuvering thru the issue of Duterte's "colorful language" and a desire to convince the general Filipino public that this is the heart of the problem. In fact the two are components of the push for a more independent Philippines.

Frankly, that capability has long been delayed by timid Philippine presidents who did not dare to cross the line. Duterte did. For that he faces the danger of being removed from political scene because it's the common perception that what America wants, America gets."

Is it?

I agree with PFVR that the Duterte administration's next 100 days (or the rest of his term) will be much, much better, considering the entire gamut of Philippine problems, starting with poverty.

Lets get our act together.

Ooooo

OCTOBER 5, 2016
Who's Fault: The Salesmen or The Product?

Another war is going on, aside from the war on drugs, it's coming from the very vocal supporters and non-supporters of President Rody Duterte. Strong words coming from both sides are everywhere – on the internet via the social media especially at the Facebook and Twitter, the texters who are very active giving their views even on radio and on television. And there are radio stations giving air time to callers airing their sentiments and can easily be recognized if one is for or against the present administration.

There is a growing number of Filipinos who are perceived gradually realizing that they voted a leader who is fast becoming an enemy, not only inside the country but even outside of this country but no matter what, the pro-Duterte will always fight to defend their leader up to the end.

Sadly the country is again divided, as if nobody is minding the store. Blunder after blunder, mistakes not checked by people in his loop before releasing information to the public. If only some key people in the Palace are responsible enough and did their homework, 'hindi malulubak ng madalas ang Pangulo'. Although there are several times that it's the President's fault when he made remarks against people or organization due to his heightened emotion based on past experiences. But if President Duterte is quick to make harsh comments, he is also quick to apologize if he believes he committed a mistake. But pundits believe that a leader should act and talk as real head of the state. Some concerned citizens on air requested the president not to talk like he owns the nation and drag everyone in a possible war which we will all regret. Another unsolicited advice on air this afternoon was about 'respect begets respect' and cussing and loose talk could backfire.

Close to his first 100 days in office, a lot of positive things happened especially on the war on drugs despite the expected jailing of big fishes, masterminds and financiers from the underworld. Everybody were shock to see thousands of users-pushers surrendered. But in the process he is now fighting several fronts as the growing number of pros and cons are in the 'blame game' mode.

So much can be seen of these pros and cons in front of national TV as the country's legislators are investigating the so-called extra-judicial killings in aid of legislation.

On the internet, several points were given in favor of the President. The Republic Defenders, a group of respected professionals commented that- "In our 71 years of being independent, this is the first time we have a president who is not like the rest. He is genuinely pro-poor and was elected by the people without the support of traditional politicians and self serving businessmen. Some people are afraid that because of PRRD's political will and genuine desire to improve our country's plight, the oligarchs may be displaced. The traditional politicians' shenanigans may be uncovered. The narco generals and their lieutenants and the narco politicians may be unmasked. The gambling lords may lose their business. All of them run the risk of ending up in jail and/or losing their riches."

"These are the conditions that is why President Duterte is already fighting so many fronts, in various factions because he is very firm and sincere in his war on drugs and corruption that those who are hit, tends to retaliate by finding ways to topple him down or worst, assassinate him."

"PRRD is not the typical president who had to horse trade to win. Thus, he has a free hand to do as he deems best for the Philippines. This is the first time his supporters which run into the millions continue to involve themselves in the affairs of government and openly declare support for PRRD to the extent of using their own funds."

"His cabinet is composed mostly of septuagenarians, where money is no longer the main objective, but to leave legacies behind."

"He touched base with the poor specially the leftists such that for the first time, his SONA was not picketed but supported by the masses."

"PRRD is tough and walks his talk. He and his selected men cannot be bribed. Therefore, the crooked and the rich are no longer within their comfort zones."

The above-mentioned are just some of the statements observed by those in favor of the leadership of the present administration.

On the contrary, the opposite are also aired through the internet by some factions who are not in favor of what the present leadership is doing and saying.

They see the push for an independent foreign policy of the government (but in favor of China and Russia) as an "attack on the west to appease the east" particularly the country's decades-long ties with the United States and our membership with the United Nations.

It is some kind of a suicidal move to break our tie with the US by putting an end to all military exercises and in the process scrapping bilateral military agreements.

Some anti-communist groups are more fiery in their attack against PRRD claiming that " if you quack like a duck, walk like a duck, you're a duck." They said that the people should not just be vigilant every time PRRD talks but be wary of his actions.

A former communist turned nationalist warned that a possible repeat of the Bolshevik revolution, a Stalin or Castro of Cuba takeover is in the offing.

A retired military officer disclosed that it could be a combination of all scenarios. He reminded discreetly some of his friends that it could be what they call in the intelligence lingo 'painting in the west but fighting in the east'. Meaning the possible air,sea and land battle between

China and other country claimants at the South China Sea is not feasible due to so many allies war machines nearby.

But a purging from within is believed to be a possibility especially now that the PRRD administration has given the left an alliance which the left hardliners could fast-track their real agenda. He added that since the AFP and the Department of Education scrapped the ROTC military training including the hibernated Congressional Committee Against Anti-Filipino Activities, it reportedly emboldened China to recruit young Chinoys to be sleepers and trained PLA soldiers in disguise as taking their vacation in mainland China.

A scary scenario which happened in the past when the Japanese OFW's in the Philippines metamorphosed into officers of the Japanese Imperial Army when the war broke out.

The President's men were put on the spot on how and what to answer when asked if the government is really serious about his move without hurting our diplomatic ties with the US and PRRD's image in the international scene.

Really, a lot of balancing act like we are in a circus, and the Duterte administration is just beginning.

How far can the President's men and women go to defend his every word that is not music to a lot of ears, and how often they will say sorry to every mistake? And in the end, when worse comes to worst, who's fault? The salesman or the product?

May the good Lord guide PRRD to have wisdom in all his undertakings.

Ooooo

SEPTEMBER 28, 2016
Ominous

The presidency of Rodrigo Roa Duterte has its many firsts and for some it's too good to be true especially that the country's experiences from the past leaders, the recent ones were all tainted with so much irregularities and anomalies. Filipinos thought that the 'new normal' nowadays are the things that were passed on from previous administrations or could it be that the majority are just too tired and let things be as they are – the status quo.

Although netizens who are aware of the current issues are the ones who are very active in posting their views and comments of the things they strongly disagree or agree via the internet. It is a fact that the last election maximized the use of the internet in reaching out to the electorate.

Now that the 'majority' has voted a strong and brave leader, the rest has to bear with him for the rest of his six-year term or less? If one will notice that in several speeches of President Duterte, he kept on mentioning that "if he can finish his term" or "if he is still alive" to fulfill his promises. The several "ifs" that seem to make him accomplish things in a hurry and in the long run, some empty promises being made.

What is also ominous according to a psychic friend, is his use of DU30. I was reminded that most journalists writes 30 which means death or end.

Desperately wanting to finish such a huge problem like the war on drugs in a short span of time, President Duterte also visited as many military camps as possible when he has the time. Seeking the help of the military arm to fulfill his goal of a drug-free country, he promised a lot of benefits to the men in uniform and their families including a doubled monthly salary, as soon as possible. But he forgot that the government is still tied to the last administration's budget and that the huge problem of rehabilitation of hundreds of drug users/pushers is impossible to achieve and so he is perceived making commitments beyond in the process.

Our president has done this due to his heightened emotion against the drug problems but Mr. President, you have to be very careful in handling your emotions being exposed through your words, no matter how sincere you are, it will only be used against you if you fail. Sadly, most of these words were directed to officials of foreign countries and organizations. Economists and those who are not so fond with President Duterte are now blaming him for the poor performance of our 'economic fundamentals'.

With the hearings in both houses of Congress (in aid of legislation), several matters of great importance were exposed.

In his article at the Manila Times, Atty. Al Vitangcol 3rd wrote his observations – "The recent justice committee hearings in the Senate and House of Representatives revealed and made public a lot of things that were only heard from the grapevine before. Now, these things are officially out and part of the public records, by way of the Minutes of the committee hearings.

One of these disclosures is the alleged Plan B, which is to destabilize the Duterte Administration and create a scenario to oust President Rodrigo Duterte. If this will not work, then impeach President Duterte. If all else fails, then assassinate the President. Once Duterte is gone, install Vice President Leni Robredo as the new President of the Republic.

Senator Alan Peter Cayetano revived talks, this time officially during the Senate Committee on Justice and Human Rights hearing, of the Liberal Party's alleged Plan B to unseat President Duterte.

My insight says otherwise. The supposed Plan B will not prosper and will not muster the support of the people and the military. However, even before Plan B could take off, the groundwork for "Plan D" has already been laid."

And what is this Plan D all about?

Plan D is the full military takeover of the government in the event of President Duterte's sudden departure before 2022. His sudden departure could be the result of any of these things – impeachment, forced ouster by foreign states, assassination, or natural death.

In his speech before the 9th Infantry Brigade, the President said in part (while showing and waving the third "narco-list"), "How can I handle this? I cannot just arrest them and kill them. That is nothing. I do not like Martial Law. This will destroy your children, or your grandchildren and the next generation. That is why we are ready to die ... because they are not safe anymore."

The President admitted that it is the technicality of the law that makes it hard for him to deal swiftly with the problem of illegal drugs and criminality.

He added, "if that problem outlasts me, for whatever reason, mamatay ako, matanggal, oh ano sa buhay na ito. Sinabi ko sa inyo, isa sa mga opisyal, do not, do not abandon. Resolbahin ninyo ang problema na iyan kasi sisirain ang Pilipinas niyan." (If that problem outlasts me, for whatever reason, I died, I am removed from this life.

I say to you, I said to one of your officers, do not, do not abandon it. Resolve this problem because this will destroy the Philippines.)

He ended his speech by extolling the troops to act on their own in this wise.

It is my opinion that if President Duterte will suddenly be gone, then the military will act on its own and take control of the government. (Atty. Al Vitangcol)

Yes, there are a lot of possibilities if worse comes to worst and we suddenly become a leaderless country. But for now let us give our support to President Duterte but be very vigilant and carry a lot of prayers in our heart that such eventuality will not happen because all of us will be dragged into the pits. Let's hope that will not be our destination. Sadly, it is now rumored that some of the people in the President's loop are not thinking the same and few were concerned about is "what's in it for me" coupled with arrogance. They should gather their act together and make his presidency lasts up to the last day.

Ooooo

SEPTEMBER 21, 2016
China's 5th Column

America's overall image around the world remains largely positive. Across the nations surveyed (excluding the U.S.), a median of 69% hold a favorable opinion of the U.S., while just 24% express an unfavorable view. However, there is significant variation among regions and countries.

In the aftermath of the Great Recession, many foreign commentators including Americans remarked that the era of U.S. dominance of the global economy and position as sole superpower were at an end. However, in the intervening years, a sustained economic recovery in the U.S. has bolstered its leadership credentials, and in the current survey, about twice as many people worldwide say that the U.S., and not China, is the world's leading economy.

Nonetheless, global public perception continue to express the view that China either has or eventually will replace the U.S. as the leading superpower. (Source Pew Research Center)

America's image is mostly positive among the Asian nations polled. Among these countries surveyed was the Philippines with an 85 percent score in 2014 and 92 percent in 2015 according to the Global Attitudes Project of Pew Research Center in Washington DC. People were asked "Do you have a favorable or unfavorable view of the US?"

Methinks we still maintain a high percentage score up to this moment with a favorable view of the US in spite of the 'bullish' attitude of our president towards some high-ranking American officials. Some observers believe that President Rody Duterte, in the midst of his balancing act between the US and China, is actually showing that he favors China more.

But the present administration has to be wary because the current war on drugs not only in and out of the largest prison camp like the National Bilibid Prison involves some confirmed Triad gang Chinese nationals. And the perennial problem in the South China Sea over territories that we won from the Hague's Permanent Court of Arbitration is not being recognized and respected by China, and in the process, our fishermen are still being 'harassed'.

The perception is that the US is still the better 'devil' that we know than the red Chinese who has exported their underworld ops to our country instead of being grateful to the Filipinos who gave them comfort several times and second home where they now become the 'novo' rich.

We have to be wary of China's sleepers (hybernated spies) and DPA (deep penetration agents) pretending to be part of the social media and our society. They are just waiting in the wings to take over anytime.

Remember the Japanese agents in the Philippines before the second world war. Most of them are lowly employees, drivers, gardeners, small time merchants, etc. but when the war erupted, they metamorphosed and our parents were shocked to know that their neighbor was a military officer of the Japanese Imperial Army.

It could be worst this time, these pro-Beijing ethnic Chinese basically control everything. Many politicians, key government functionaries, even some officials in our AFP, PNP, judiciary and the 'church' are now in their pockets.

Be vigilant always. These sleepers are now bold enough to attack us. The mere fact that even their Facebook pages and social media accounts are fictitious.

And I got this message from a rich friend from China- "it's a pity that overseas Chinese especially in the Philippines thought that China can save them in a nuke war. We have more billionaires here in China not flaunting their wealth nor included at Forbes Magazine richest. If China's nuke hit the Philippines, they will be part of the so called collateral damage whether they like it or not."

Who do we believe now? Beware of the propaganda machines. The program is on.

Touche!

Ooooo

SEPTEMBER 14, 2016
Live Bullet War Exercises, A Prelude To A Real War?

The fifth annual China-Russia naval drill (that will go on for eight days) started last Monday, featuring stalwarts from both navies in action at the eastern waters of Zhanjiang, in Guangdong province, the HQ of the People's Liberation Army (PLA) Navy Nanhai Fleet.

Considering this is the first time that the Joint Sea is happening in the South China Sea, apocalyptic alarms from the usual suspects could not be more predictable – and thoroughly dismissed by the Beijing leadership. (Pepe Escobar @Reuters online)

Usually, the joint military exercise between Russia and China took place in the Sea of Japan also known as East Asia.

What a coincidence that a US military drill named 'Variant Shield', 2,000 miles to the east, the US military around the Pacific gathered for a two weeks drill with 18,000 personnel, 180 aircrafts and USS Ronald Reagan aircraft carrier.

Overheard that President Rody Duterte said that any possible miscalculation during such naval exercise in the contested area, using live ammunitions at that, might lead to a regional conflict. Ominous?

But can we blame President Duterte by thinking such possibility might happen? Actually there are other observers who feel the same and fear the same might just occur if either side will not be careful during the military exercises.

It is in this context that we should allow and continue our military relationship with the US, whether we like it or not, our status as a treaty ally of the US did not start last June 30, 2016. With the cooperation of our past leaders (others were collaborators) with Uncle Sam in the name of national security and to preserve democracy, various treaties were signed.

Revisiting some of these treaties by the present administration will somehow correct the lopsided parts where we are being shortchanged and the fact that such agreements should be ratified by the proper institutions like our Congress and not just the Executive branch.

Of course we welcome the statement of President Duterte of an independent foreign policy for the country but it should be handled with utmost diplomacy without hurting our existing allies for so many years now. And like any policy, it should be without bias and always for the common good and not only for the favored few. Pres. Duterte if he will do it right, can use this as a leverage and his charting an independent policy will be a good bargaining point with the Americans and with China. A balancing act that should be supported by the people.

In the course of the President's balancing act locally and globally, he should listen to the Filipino people who believe in him and in what he can do for the good of this nation if he doesn't want to be called a dictator in the making.

In his article, Duterte's 'shock and awe' diplomacy, La Salle professor Richard Javad Heydarian cited some of his observations on the President's kind of diplomacy and his attitude towards certain matters – "For those, who have underestimated his ability to reconfigure existing relations with the Southeast Asian country's most enduring ally, the United States, the past two weeks have been a rude awakening. Rapidly consolidating power over key institutions of the state, and backed up by robust support among various civil society groups, Duterte is in a position to redirect the Philippines' foreign policy like none of his predecessors."

Dr. Erick San Juan, D.Litt.   **116**

"I'm really a rude person. I'm enjoying my last time as a rude person," Duterte famously promised earlier. "When I become president, when I take my oath of office . . . there will be a metamorphosis." It was a statement of re-assurance that compelled many to (mistakenly) presume that Duterte's tough campaign-period rhetoric – including those directed at America – was nothing but a clever gimmick.

So when Duterte embarked on his global diplomatic debut, attending the Association of Southeast Asian Nations (ASEAN) summit, many were expecting a more subdued and statesmanlike Duterte. Instead, the world witnessed a Hyde and Jekyll diplomatic behavior. Duterte, who accepted the Philippines' (rotational) chairmanship of the regional group, gracefully embraced his fellow Asian leaders, who appreciated his pragmatism on the South China Sea disputes and relations with China, while going on the offensive against the United States President Barack Obama, who was on his final official trip to Asia.

After uttering what appeared as expletives against the American president, the much-anticipated Obama-Duterte bilateral meeting was cancelled. Shortly after, amid growing panic over a potential diplomatic meltdown, Manila released a statement of "regret", while the Obama administration reiterated that U.S.-Philippine relations remain "rock solid." Duterte clarified that his foul-mouthed remarks weren't directed at Obama, who reassured his Filipino partners that he didn't take Duterte's insulting remarks personally.

Yet, just when everyone thought that the damage control efforts were bearing fruit, Duterte once again went on the offensive. And most recently has even asked, albeit rhetorically so far, American special forces in the troubled region of Mindanao to get out of the country. He has also made it clear that he is setting his sights on more robust ties, including military, with eastern powers of Russia and China. In fact, Duterte is expected to embark on his state visit to China, a first by any Filipino leader, in coming weeks. In a span of months, Philippine-US relations have gone from special and sacrosanct to uncertain and jittery. And this seems to be the new normal in one of the most intimate and enduring bilateral relations on the planet."

Are we going to end the most enduring bilateral relations that we had for years now and start a new bilateral relations with China?

Methinks it's better to deal with the 'devil' we know than a perceived 'angel' with the same clothes and interest like the demon. I hope Pres. Duterte will be in the right direction to correct our misfortunes.

Just asking.

Ooooo

SEPTEMBER 7, 2016
Hegemony by Design

When you study how the United States goes to war, there is a prevalent, though not perfect, pattern. The triggering event is often a sudden crisis that galvanizes popular opinion and becomes the immediate occasion for military intervention, but subsequently is exposed as a misguided perception or outright fabrication. (Source: Joseph Ellis, Los Angeles Times, 7-6-2014)

Such pattern, most of the time is considered as false flag operation by a lot of pundits where a superpower wanted to maintain a unipolar world – hegemony over sovereign states. Gradually this 'op' is losing its clout because world leaders are now beginning to realize that humankind has to shift to multipolar world.

Of course the mighty 'Uncle' will not allow such move and so is the containment of Russia and China, countries advocating a multipolar world. Their effort ranges from economic to military cooperation. With the initiative of both Russia and China, there are several cooperation, coalitions and organizations created to counter the hegemony of a single power over the world. Despite that these two big powers don't really trust each other, using the principle of- 'The enemy of my enemy is my friend', they have to cooperate with each other in some ways to protect their interests.

To name some, from the article of Pepe Escobar published in the Information Clearing House – "Slowly but surely — see for instance the possibility of an ATM (Ankara-Tehran-Moscow) coalition in the making — global power continues to insist on shifting East. That goes beyond Russia's pivoting to Asia; Germany's industrialists are just waiting for the right political conjunction, before the end of the decade, to also pivot to Asia, conforming a BMB (Berlin-Moscow-Beijing) coalition.

Germany already rules over Europe. The only way for a global trade power to solidify its reach is to go East. NATO member Germany, with a GDP that outstrips the UK, Canada, Australia and New Zealand, is not even allowed to share information with the "Five Eyes" secret cabal.

Russian President Vladimir Putin, years ago, was keen on a Lisbon-to-Vladivostok emporium. He may eventually be rewarded — delayed gratification?— by BMB, a trade/economic union that, combined with the Chinese-driven One Belt, One Road (OBOR), will eventually dwarf and effectively replace the dwindling post-WWII Anglo-Saxon crafted/controlled international order.

This inexorable movement East underscores all the interconnections — and evolving connectivity — related to the New Silk Roads, the Shanghai Cooperation Organization (SCO), the BRICS's New Development Bank (NDB), the Asian Infrastructure Investment Bank (AIIB), the Eurasia Economic Union (EEU). The crux of RC, the Russia China strategic partnership, is to make the multipolar, post-Atlantic world happen. Or, updating Ezra Pound, to Make It New.

Such luminary ideologues as Dr. Zbig "Grand Chessboard" Brzezinski — foreign policy mentor to President Barack Obama — are supremely dejected.

When Brzezinski looks at progressive Eurasia integration, he simply cannot fail to detect how those "three grand imperatives of imperial geostrategy" he outlined in 'The Grand Chessboard' are simply dissolving; "to prevent collusion and maintain security dependence among the vassals, to keep tributaries pliant and protected, and to keep the barbarians from coming together."

Those GCC vassals — starting with the House of Saud — are now terrified about their own security; same with the hysteric Baltics. Tributaries are not pliant anymore — and that includes an array of Europeans. The "barbarians" coming together are in fact old civilizations — China, Persia, Russia — fed up with upstart-controlled unipolarity.

Unsurprisingly, to "contain" RC, defined as "potentially threatening" (the Pentagon considers the threats are existential) Brzezinski suggests — what else — Divide and Rule; as in "containing the least predictable but potentially the most likely to overreach." Still he doesn't know which is which; "Currently, the more likely to overreach is Russia, but in the longer run it could be China."

The board game will have to reach a point where a change of players and rules of the game be created in order to prevent a world war. Although we have to accept that the change of players on the side of the single superpower will affect the pivot from unipolar to multipolar, or worst to stage a war or not.

"In many aspects, not much has changed from 24 years ago when, only three months after the dissolution of the USSR, the Pentagon's Defense Planning Guidance proclaimed.

"Our first objective is to prevent the reemergence of a new rival...This requires that we endeavor to prevent any hostile power from dominating a region whose resources would, under consolidated control, be sufficient to generate global power. These regions include Western Europe, East Asia, the territory of the former Soviet Union and southwest Asia."

Talk about a prescient road map of what's happening right now; the "rival", hostile power is actually two powers involved in a strategic partnership: Russia and China.

Compounding this Pentagon nightmare, the endgame keeps drawing near; the next manifestations and reverberations of the never-ending 2008 financial crisis may eventually torpedo the fundamentals of the global "order" — as in the petrodollar racket/tributary scam.

There will be blood. Hillary Clinton smells it already — from Syria to Iran to the South China Sea. The question is whether she — and virtually the whole Beltway establishment behind her — will be mad enough to provoke Russia and China and buy a one-way ticket to post-MAD (Mutual Assured Destruction) territory."

The programmed world war is coming as designed. Can the emerging multipolar world prevent it from happening? Scary indeed.

Ooooo

AUGUST 31, 2016
China-phobia

On September 4 to 5, China's tourist hub of Hangzhou will be this year's venue of the G-20 meeting and China's President Xi Jinping is hoping to cement its standing as a global power when it host leaders from the world's biggest economies. But China suspects the West and its allies will try to deny Beijing what it sees as its rightful place on the international stage.

While China wants to make sure its highest profile event of the year goes off successfully, Pres. Xi will be under pressure at home to ensure he is strong in the face of challenges to his authority on issues like the South China Sea, going by reports in state media.

China has already made it clear that it does not want such matters overshadowing the meeting, which will be attended by U.S. President Barack Obama, Japanese Prime Minister Shinzo Abe and other world leaders.

State media has given great play to the idea that G-20 is for China to show leadership in shaping global governance rules and forging ahead with sustainable global growth, with the official People's Daily saying this could be one of the G-20's most fruitful ever get-togethers. (Source: Reuters published at www.dailystar.com)

Can the G-20 meeting in China help boost Xi's nation's image or his own image in the world community of nations? The mere fact that no matter how he tries to put major issues on the back burner, the heat will be felt and people will be reacting in the process.

One such issue is the Permanent Court of Arbitration ruling on the territorial disputes in the South China Sea. Although the decision has favored the Philippines, there are still incidents of Filipino fishermen being bullied by some Chinese coast guard. The world knows that China never accepted the decision and stubbornly insisted its claim based on their history. And in the process continuously building up structures in the reclaimed land despite protests from its neighbors and other countries passing in the region with their cargos.

Another one is with Japan on the East China Sea, again a disputed territory that has been going on for quite some time now and the issue will continue as long as China will insist on bilateral talks in solving the problem which is not what Japan wants.

These issues no matter how vague, could somehow affect the meeting of the member countries of the G-20. Of course, the main agenda – economy which is not doing well as per all the major economies of the world. And no matter how China manipulates the news on the real economic condition of their country, the truth will surface anyway.

Actually the following 'incidents' will show how China is doing in the economic front.

Was it China-phobia that recently forced Britain and Australia to postpone or cancel Chinese investment in their sensitive sectors? The two countries seem to be genuinely concerned about national security issues linked to these investments while China dismisses their fears as unfounded and absurd.

In its two opinion pieces published on August 11 and 18, Xinhua News, the Chinese government's official press agency, accused Great Britain and Australia of China-phobia and warned both countries that their China-phobia could damage cooperation with Beijing.

Though China-phobia or Sino-phobia has long surfaced in some circles, this is probably the first time a key Chinese news agency has publicly mentioned it.

This came following the United Kingdom's postponement of a $23.5 billion nuclear power station project at Hinkley Point, to which China General Nuclear Power(CGN) is supposed to finance a third, and Australia's rejection of the sale of Ausgrid, its largest electricity network, to Chinese state-owned State Grid Corp and Hong Kong-based Cheung Kong Infrastructure.

China's muscle-reflecting and its rather arrogant attitudes, e.g. "you're wrong and we're right" or "you're a small country and we're a big country" views, have stirred uneasiness and resentment in some countries.

Though it is unsure whether they have actually transformed into "China-phobia", concerns or even fears over China's intentions, behaviors and investments exist in Great Britain, Australia and perhaps in other countries.

Those apprehensions also play a key role in defining their relations with China. As shown in the editorial of the Independent mentioned above, China's behavior in the international sphere, e.g. its assertive and coercive behavior in the South China Sea, affect perceptions and apprehensions of the UK's government and public.

This demonstrates that like material powers, e.g. economic and military capabilities, non-material factors, perceptions and reputations, are also influential in international politics. (Source: Why some countries are concerned over Chinese investment by Xuan Loc Doan, August 29, 2016 in Asia Times)

These two countries have their concerns and doubts on how they will deal with China because on the surface no matter how China extends its soft power operations, there are still underlying issues that has to be taken into consideration especially when it comes to national security.

Lastly, China's 'growing mountain of debt' as what was reported by Bloomberg that "Some prominent investors are worried about China's debt. George Soros sees an 'eerie resemblance' between conditions in China now and those in the U.S. leading up to the financial crisis in 2008. It's similarly fueled by credit growth and an eventually unsustainable extension of credit," Soros told the Asia Society in New York in April.

BlackRock Chief Executive Officer Laurence Fink was asked about China's mounting debt on Bloomberg TV in May. "We all have to be worried about it," Fink said, adding that he remains bullish on China's economy in the long run.

And in June a Goldman Sachs report warned that the country's large and unaccounted-for shadow-banking activities raised concern "about China's underlying credit problems and sustainability risk."

Indeed, many segments of the Chinese economy have taken on considerable debt, especially since the global financial crisis. Over the past decade, total debt grew 465 percent. Debt rose to 247 percent of gross domestic product in 2015, from 160 percent in 2005. Bloomberg Intelligence breaks China's total debt into four components: bank, corporate, government, and household.

This isn't to say that China doesn't have some serious problems. Growth is slowing and the economy needs major restructuring. There will be winners and losers and turmoil in the market. Shadow-banking activities add another risk. It isn't certain that the government will handle the challenges in the next decade as deftly as it has in the past. The country's economy is far larger and more complex.

Fortunately for the rest of the world, China has a high savings rate. Capital controls aren't fully lifted, making capital flight difficult. The government has almost complete control of the banking industry. In addition, China's listed banks get about 70 percent of their funds from deposits. In comparison, U.S. investment banks in 2008 relied heavily on short-term money-market funding.

Such circumstances make it unlikely that China's debt will spark a global crisis in the near future."

Indeed, a lot of expectations and worries will come at China's doorstep as it welcomes this year's G-20 meeting. Can it help China project the image it desperately wanted? Let's wait and see, especially how the Federal Reserve meeting on September 20-21 will play on and most likely will increase its interest rate which could create a sliding domino effect for the world in the process.

Ooooo

AUGUST 24, 2016
Don't Be Pessimistic

Our country is once again divided as various issues confront us, vital to our day to day lives. With the personalities up front raging word wars, so are the people especially the netizens. After the initial two-day hearing on extra-judicial killings at the senate chaired by Senator Leila de Lima, several points were cleared by the PNP chief Gen. Ronald dela Rosa on the war on drugs. After the so many hours spent on the senate hearing in aid of legislation, the 'war' continues and so are the killings.

The so-called war on drugs is concentrated mostly on the poor drug users and pushers, the public is asking time and again, where are the 'big fish'? So many questions and the answers were so limited and very evasive. Like most killed are reportedly 'assets' of some scalawags in uniform who wanted to silence them and not to spill the beans. The suspected drug lord Peter Lim and family already left through a private jet for unknown destination. The case of father and son tandem – Mayor Rolly and son Kerwin Espinosa, some observers believed that they were treated like VIPs and were released eventually. Reason? No case to file against them, yet. The one was met by the President himself in Malacanang and the other one even stayed in the PNP's white house. Pundits believe that if these are the ways the 'big fishes' were being treated, can we blame the public for asking why such biased treatment is being done if the present leadership is really waging this war on drugs seriously without fear and favor?

Remember we are not alone in this war, at the senate hearing it was mentioned by the Commission on Human Rights head Chito Gascon that there is a possibility that the International Criminal Court can investigate and may impose sanction on the responsible individuals who allowed the rampant extra-judicial killings. In other words, the people in the government should be wary on how to conduct their operations because we are being watched by the international community. Whether the President likes it or not, we are a member in a community of nations who are outside the box looking in for any possible violation of human rights.

But we have to remind the Commission on Human Rights and the United Nations that some alleged 'salvaging' were executed before the Duterte administration.

Yes, we are one with the President in upholding our sovereign rights as an independent nation but diplomacy dictates that we should respect people and organizations who are doing their jobs to maintain peace and harmony among sovereign states. And if we as a member of such group, we should respect and follow its rules for the protection of our citizenry.

As we wrote before, the present leadership of President Duterte is faced with a lot of problems and issues handed down from the past administrations. One is the communist insurgency which is now conducting the peace talks in Oslo, Norway. Some observers are asking why it had to be outside the country, this peace talk?

Like what former National Security Secretary Bert Gonzales said in his article that was published at the Manila Times – "Why can't the peace talks be held where they are now? Government can easily provide suitable facilities for talks within their detention area. For those in Utrecht, except for Jose Maria Sison, who continues to be on the international terrorist list, they have been freely traveling to the Philippines, anyway."

"Sison claims to be a mere consultant in the talks. His absence should not really matter. The Norwegian third party facilitators certainly will not mind enjoying Manila hospitality. What is important is that doing the talks here will not require the Philippines to bend its laws."

"It is a good time to confront some communist beliefs that threaten national security. Many communists all over the world went through this in their respective countries, where they have now become important political players and are effectively co-existing with other ideologically founded political forces. The talks will not bring peace as intended if these beliefs are not confronted and reconciled with once and for all."

The peace talks with the communist group is just one of the so many government tasks, there is also the problem with the MNLF and the MILF and the possible new BBL version to reckon with. And the continuing military confrontations with the bandits of the Abu Sayyaf Group.

That's not all, even the nagging question of the burial of former president Ferdinand Marcos, whether it should be buried in the Libingan ng mga Bayani or not really divides the people. But as of this writing, the Supreme Court came out with its status quo anti order for twenty days on the fate of the Marcos burial. It was put on hold until the day of the oral arguments next month.

We have to remind our people that I was part of the entourage from Hawaii to Ilocos Norte of the former President Ferdinand Marcos body and he has long been buried beside his beloved mother, Dona Josefa. What many people are seeing in Ilocos is the refrigerated wax replica of Marcos patterned to Lenin's open museum at the Red Square in Kremlin that we saw during the visit of former President Fidel Ramos in Russia.

These are just among the so many hurdles that President Digong had to face day in and day out. Maybe the severity and scope of these problems had made the president looks uneasy sometimes and tend to say words that later on regrets as saying. For whatever its worth, he is the elected president and we should support his administration but not to forget also that we are still in a democracy with all its flaws, let us all be vigilant and pray for the best that this nation will survive despite all the problems.

Ooooo

AUGUST 17, 2016
Will All Hell Break Loose Soon?

Or Who Will Strike First?

If the world thinks that after the PCA's (Permanent Court of Arbitration) ruling on the territorial disputes between the Philippines and China, conflict in the region or a possible war will be farfetched, think again.

Despite the diplomatic talks between the US and China and military to military arrangement like the recent meeting between US Army chief of staff Gen. Mark Milley and China's Peoples Liberation Army Gen. Li Zuocheng Tuesday, August 16 in Beijing, the war cycle is still on. In the recent study from the Pentagon's think tank RAND Corporation - War with China, Thinking Through the Unthinkable, it stated that "premeditated war between the United States and China is very unlikely, but the danger that a mishandled crisis could trigger hostilities cannot be ignored. Thus, while neither state wants war, both states' militaries have plans to fight one."

How can one avoid the crisis (by design) if it is a programmed one and yes it can be delayed but it will happen whether we like it or not. Unfortunately, in this case, it could be sooner than we think.

As the present administration is busy solving problems here and there, even the problem with China using the backdoor (so to speak), according to RAND's report, the US-China war could start in the East China Sea. In this case, the Japan-China territorial dispute at the Senkaku islands could be the trigger that will start the war between US and China. The bad part of this 'studied scenario' is the glaring reality of the US virtual military bases here via EDCA (Enhanced Defense Cooperation Agreement) and before we know it, we are waging the American war against China just because we allowed it or should we say, our past leaders did it as slaves to a perceived master.

Another irony (according to RAND Corporation) is the use of conventional warfare if ever the US-China war will happen. No nukes! Seriously?

In this age, if one is in the league of nuclear-armed superpowers, and not to use nuclear weapons if threatened or in the line of fire and in the middle of a war, is insane.

To continue the RAND study it states – "As Chinese anti-access and area-denial (A2AD) capabilities improve, the United States can no longer be so certain that war would follow its plan and lead to decisive victory. This analysis illuminates various paths a war with China could take and their possible consequences.

Technological advances in the ability to target opposing forces are creating conditions of conventional counterforce, whereby each side has the means to strike and degrade the other's forces and, therefore, an incentive to do so promptly, if not first. This implies fierce early exchanges, with steep military losses on both sides, until one gains control. At present, Chinese losses would greatly exceed U.S. losses, and the gap would only grow as fighting persisted. But, by 2025, that gap could be much smaller. Even then, however, China could not be confident of gaining military advantage, which suggests the possibility of a prolonged and destructive, yet inconclusive, war. In that event, nonmilitary factors — economic costs, internal political effects, and international reactions — could become more important.

Political leaders on both sides could limit the severity of war by ordering their respective militaries to refrain from swift and massive conventional counterforce attacks. The resulting restricted, sporadic fighting could substantially reduce military losses and economic harm. This possibility underscores the importance of firm civilian control over wartime decision-making and of communication between capitals. At the same time, the United States can prepare for a long and severe war by reducing its vulnerability to Chinese A2AD forces and developing plans to ensure that economic and international consequences would work to its advantage.

Both sides would suffer large military losses in a severe conflict. In 2015, U.S. losses could be a relatively small fraction of forces committed, but still significant;

Chinese losses could be much heavier than U.S. losses and a substantial fraction of forces committed.

This gap in losses will shrink as Chinese A2AD improves. By 2025, U.S. losses could range from significant to heavy; Chinese losses, while still very heavy, could be somewhat less than in 2015, owing to increased degradation of U.S. strike capabilities.

China's A2AD will make it increasingly difficult for the United States to gain military-operational dominance and victory, even in a long war."

Now they are talking about a severe long war. A perpetual war? God forbid!

We have to be ready and if there is still time correct the mistakes of the past leaders and demand what is due us from our treaty allies if war really is inevitable.

Ooooo

AUGUST 9, 2016
After Ramos, Narco-Politics Proliferate

"I don't want to defy economic logic and say supply creates demand, but to a certain extent it feels that way," Steven Dudley, co-founder of InSight Crime, a foundation that studies organized crime in Latin America.

Because as long as there are people willing to produce and supply the illicit drugs to users and would-be users, demands will be created in the process for something that is very addicting creating the demand would be that easy.

This perennial problem of drug trafficking tackled at the meeting of diplomats and top officials from governments around the world in mid-April this year at United Nations headquarters in New York to discuss what to do about the global drug problem. Over the course of four days and multiple discussions, the assembled dignitaries vowed to take a more comprehensive approach to the issue than in years past — but they also decided to keep waging the war on drugs.

The "outcome document" adopted during the UN General Assembly's special session (UNGASS) calls for countries to "prevent and counter" drug-related crime by disrupting the "illicit cultivation, production, manufacturing, and trafficking" of cocaine, heroin, methamphetamine, and other substances banned by international law. The document also reaffirmed the UN's "unwavering commitment" to "supply reduction and related measures."

Yet according to the UN's own data, the supply-oriented approach to fighting drug trafficking has been a failure of epic proportions. Last May, the United Nations Office on Drugs and Crime (UNODC) issued its 2015 World Drug Report, which shows that — despite billions of dollars spent trying to eradicate illicit crops, seize drug loads, and arrest traffickers — more people than ever before are getting high.

The UNODC conservatively estimated that in 2013, the most recent year for which data is available, 246 million people worldwide, or 1 out of 20 individuals between the ages of 15 and 64, used an illicit drug, an increase of 3 million people over the previous year. More alarmingly, 27 million people were characterized as "problem drug users." Only one out of every six of these problem users had access to any sort of addiction treatment. (Source: The Golden Age of Drug Trafficking: How Meth, Cocaine, and Heroin Move Around the World by Keegan Hamilton, April 2016)

The efforts of the Duterte administration on its war on drugs for its first month has already shown how this drug problem has deeply penetrated the very roots of our society. Unfortunately, President Rody Duterte said that the so-called big fish is not here in the country. Supplies are just coming in from abroad and the contacts here – the drug lords and its minions are the ones selling the "merchandize" to the locals.

How to stop drug trafficking is the number one problem now because experts believe that the rise of globalization and high-speed and hi-tech form of communications made the trafficking or transactions of illegal drugs much easier.

Of the three most used illegal drugs - meth, cocaine, and heroin, it is the methamphetamine (or shabu) that is very popular here in the country.

According to Hamilton in his article, demand for methamphetamine has soared since the UN's last drug summit in 1998, and it has become one of the most popular

— and profitable — illicit substances in nearly every corner of the world. From Australia and Asia to Africa and North America, meth is the poster drug for the global narco economy.

The quantities of meth confiscated by authorities over the past decade reflect its rise. According to the UNODC, global meth seizures nearly quadrupled from 24 tons in 2008 to 114 tons in 2012. Meth seizures in Mexico increased from 341 kilograms in 2008 to 44 tons in 2012. In Australia, meth seizures in Australia soared by more than 400 percent in a single year, climbing from 426 kilograms in 2011 to 2,269 kilos in 2012.

In Asia, meth is primarily produced in China, where the precursor chemicals needed to synthesize the drug are abundant, and in the lawless Golden Triangle region of Myanmar and Laos. Douglas, the UNODC rep in Southeast Asia, said that "crystal meth is exploding in the region." According to the UNODC's preliminary estimate, 25 tons of meth were seized last year across the region.

Douglas said part of meth's appeal for drug traffickers is the relatively low startup and overhead costs. Producing heroin requires paying hundreds of farmers to tend crops that can produce only a limited amount of poppy gum per harvest. For meth, it takes only a shipment of relatively easy-to-obtain chemicals and a little bit of scientific knowhow. The drug can be shipped to countries like Australia, which offers the highest price per kilo of meth anywhere in the world, and sold for an enormous profit.

But for the most part, the chemicals used to make the world's meth originate in China, where a booming pharmaceutical industry manufactures all the raw ingredients to produce "ice," the common name for glassy shards of high-purity crystal meth. According to data presented by the Chinese government at UNGASS, the country seized a whopping 20,338 tons of meth precursor chemicals from 2009 to 2015. Busts have shown that individual villages are capable of producing enormous quantities of the drug. On a single day in 2013 in Boshe, a village northeast of Hong Kong on the Chinese mainland, authorities seized three tons of meth and more than 100 tons of precursors.

"With crystal meth, the leader appears to be China, but they also produce significant amounts in the Philippines and in Indonesia, and also to some extent in Myanmar,"

Douglas said. "But what we've seen in recent years is industrial-scale production from a few labs in China."

In 1995, i wrote an article, 'After FVR, Narco-Politics in the Offing', published by several newspapers. I'm now vindicated.

It is about time that all of us should be ever vigilant and help the Duterte government to put a STOP to this drug menace and really pray harder that his administration will have the strength to continuously fight this 'war' and that he may live longer to see its success. May God bless us all.

Ooooo

AUGUST 2, 2016
The Left, Who's the Real Leader?

More power to President Rodrigo Duterte and his goal to unify the nation since day one of his term, a sweeping unity making waves across the political spectrum but unfortunately it was not rightly reciprocated by the other party from the left. The President's offer of a unilateral ceasefire to the CPP-NPA-NDF announced during his State of the Nation Address was recently cancelled.

According to reports, President Duterte issued the ultimatum after a government militia man was killed and four others were wounded in what the military said was an ambush by the NPA (New Peoples Army) in the southern province of Compostela Valley last Wednesday. The rebels owned up to the attack, but said they were thwarting an Army offensive.

The response from the communist party was later given after three hours from the deadline. It is now clear that local NPA's are not the ideologues that we know in the past. There appears to be 'phantom' leaders for every faction within. They could be corrupt politicians, scalawags in uniform, dubious businessmen in the provinces and covert power blocs. Even Joma Sison does not control the local combatants. I don't even believe that he has the real say in that NDF(National Democratic Front) office in Utrecht. So why talk with a Christian for National Liberation inspired NDF?

Historically, PKP (Partido Komunista ng Pilipinas) was infiltrated by foreign agents like US clandestine operator William Pomeroy and even the so called 'muscovites'. Pomeroy studied in UP, met and married Celia.

Taken from their website CPP   (Communist Party of the Philippines), the Philippine Revolution Web Central, this is what they say about Pomeroy.

"It is clear why sharp attention has been given to Pomeroy. He has been the most valuable among the Lava revisionist renegades in spreading in the Philippines and abroad counter-revolutionary revisionist ideas. His writings have been published and circulated by the Soviet, American and Philippine revisionist renegades."

"Pomeroy is liable to have spread noxious ideas more than the Lavas themselves, the dynastic chieftains of the Philippine revisionist renegades, whose writings are sparse and crude. As a matter of fact, his writings are often quoted and cited by the Lava revisionist renegades who look up to him as some sort of ideological authority."

Among the Lava revisionist renegades, Pomeroy enjoys today the status of being the most trusted agent of Soviet social-imperialism. Under the cover of revisionist phrase-mongering, he also exercises his role as a special agent of U.S. imperialism. There is ample proof to show that he has been an undercover agent of U.S. imperialism, with the specific task of sabotaging the Philippine revolutionary movement.

His counter-revolutionary record is well-known in the Philippines. He collaborated with the notorious anti-communist Luis Taruc in writing the "autobiography" of betrayal, Born of the People. Under the pretext of gathering material for this book, he gathered intelligence data for U.S. imperialism. At the same time, he glorified Taruc in a sleek maneuver to spread counter-revolutionary ideas and the black line of capitulationism. To keep himself planted in the old merger party, he followed the Jose-Jesus Lava clique in its shifts from Right opportunism to "Left" opportunism.

After giving himself up to the enemy in the course of Operation "Four Roses" in 1952, he spent time in prison only to be part of the reactionary government's campaign to break the spirit of political prisoners and sponge for information that filtered in from the revolutionary mass movement. He wrote in prison the first draft of the pessimistic book, The Forest, despite the objections of others. It was upon the intercession of the U.S. government that he was released from prison in late 1961, a decade ahead of the release of those who had been sentenced like him to life imprisonment at the least. His release was in line with the U.S. imperialist support for the splitting activities of the Khrushchov revisionist renegade clique in the international communist movement. His ability to write opportunist trash qualified him for a new task from his U.S. imperialist master. (Pomeroy's Portrait: Revisionist Renegade, April 22, 1972)

There is so much to learn from history. This is the reason why we are being faced with this perennial problem created by the so called communist rebels. Even the late President Ferdinand Marcos created his own clandestine operation of leftists through the late General Galileo Kintanar then of ISAFP but some of his people used them in extracurricular and illegal activities and blamed the NPA.

Same thing happened to the late Popoy Lagman's Alex Boncayao Brigade. At first it was instrumental in the killing of scalawags in uniform but in his last days he got worried that his ABB was being used and tagged as behind some criminal activities.

And now we have the leadership of an action man who will do whatever it takes to unify the nation peacefully, we hope and pray that with the support of the whole Filipino populace, such peace and unity can be achieved.

For the other questions that still unanswered in the course of understanding the so-called 'reds' like - how was the NDF created without the sanction of the Politburo of the CPP/NPA? And why was PKP dismantled and metamorphosed into CPP without the approval of the hierarchy of PKP/HMB(Hukbong Mapagpalaya ng Bayan)? Who are the puppet masters and puppets behind the scene? Is Benito Tiamzon the real head of our local communists? Who is George Madlos of NPA in Mindanao working for? What was the real participation of the late Jesuit priest Fr. Jose 'Derp' Blanco of Ateneo in the recruitment of former UP Professors Jose Ma. Sison and Nur Misuari to destabilize the Marcos regime? Please read my book DOSSIERS, to know more. It will be out in the market very soon. Also read my other 5 conspiracy books at amazon.com.

Ooooo

JULY 26, 2016
Might is Right

In the midst of the anticipation and excitement before the much awaited State of the Nation Address (SONA) of the newly elected President Rodrigo Roa Duterte plus the euphoria over the Permanent Court of Arbitration (The Hague) ruling in favor of the Philippines against China, there were several important international meetings/conferences we overlooked.

Among these meetings were the ASEAN Foreign Ministers' Meeting (AMM) and other key ASEAN-related meetings – including East Asia Summit (EAS) Foreign Ministers' Meeting and ASEAN Regional Forum (ARF), a 27-member security dialogue – held from July 23-26 in Vientiane, Laos, ASEAN's current chair and the Trident Special Defense Symposium at the Solaire Hotel in Metro Manila.

It would be good to note that while other pro-China and the Chinese media itself seemed to project China as the underdog in the South China Sea dispute with the US siding with our country, we'll take a look again.

In the several meetings among ASEAN and non-ASEAN members, the pressure tactics employed by China were quite obvious. The mere fact that the ASEAN meetings host country of Laos (and Cambodia) both had their objections and did not join in expressing any common position on the verdict.

The objection of Cambodia and Laos, both of which are Beijing's allies and largely depend on it economically, is seen as the reason behind ASEAN' "no-statement" or "no-comment."

Beijing allegedly uses it's economic influence to lobby its two small and poor neighbors and that it exploits ASEAN's consensus, the regional grouping's modus operandi, to divide ASEAN on the South China Sea issue is universally recognized.

In 2012, ASEAN failed – for the first time in its history – to issue a joint communiqué after its AMM in Cambodia. Last month, for the second time, it was unable to agree on a joint statement after a special ASEAN-China

Foreign Ministers' Meeting in Kunming, China. In fact, it released a statement but retracted it immediately afterward.

If China succeeds in doing so, which will likely result in ASEAN's failure to issue a joint statement for the third time, the regional organization's unity, centrality and even its existence are greatly threatened.

It is very difficult, if not impossible, for the grouping to maintain its centrality in the Asia-Pacific's evolving regional architecture if it is continuously split and manipulated by a powerful outsider.

It's relevance is also greatly questioned if it ignores the South China Sea disputes, which is probably the region's biggest security concern. Moreover, four ASEAN members – Brunei, Malaysia, the Philippines and Vietnam – are directly involved in the disputes.

As it is also seeking to establish and advocate for a rules-based regional order, ASEAN cannot be silent on a ruling by an international court established under the aegis of UNCLOS.

While in another important conference at the 11th Asia-Europe Meeting (ASEM, a biennial summit of Asian and European leaders), in Ulaanbaatar, Mongolia, from July 15-16, it did not directly mention the South China Sea dispute in its closing statement.

The European Union (EU) was only able to issue a statement on the South China Sea ruling on July 15, three days after the PCA published its award. Moreover, this declaration made by Federica Mogherini, the EU's High Representative, on behalf of the 28-member bloc, did not directly name China.

The EU, which is an ardent advocate of the rule of law, failed to release an immediate and more strongly worded statement on The Hague ruling because Croatia, Hungary and Greece reportedly blocked it.

These small EU members, notably the latter, are facing many economic problems and seeking closer economic ties with Beijing.

While the EU managed to issue a common – though rather weak by its standards – statement on the PCA's award, ASEAN has conspicuously failed to do so.

China's blunt interference in the internal affairs of ASEAN, whose core principle is non-interference, has already alienated many ASEAN members. Its relationship with ASEAN is actually at a very low ebb.

Dr. Erick San Juan, D.Litt.

If China continues to pursue its long held divide and rule tactics vis-à-vis ASEAN, it will further anger many ASEAN members and push them to seek closer ties with the US, Beijing's geopolitical rival. This is not good for China in the long run.

It's a realpolitik approach or "might-makes-right" strategy to the South China Sea issue which is being questioned and scrutinized. It is also facing huge regional and international pressure that may eventually prompt it to comply – either partly or fully – with the PCA's ruling. (Source: Will China's realpolitik prevail in sea row? by Xuan Loc Doan, 7/23/16)

As to what extent thus the international community can extend its hand to China to comply with the rule of law? And with China's might makes right policy, it will continue to bully its neighbors especially the Philippines even after the PCA ruling.

As the countries in the SCS area continue to turn to the US for moral and military support, tensions in the SCS will also continue to rise. And this will never look good for China and it will assert its claim using the nine-dash line based on its so called historic rights. An end to this dispute is farfetched if China will not adhere to what is right and push for who is mightier and stronger militarily.

One have to analyze and understand why China's Xi Jinping is so stubborn and does not listen to reason.

Leaders like Xi and Turkey's Erdogan, (who reportedly hatched his own palace coup ala Ferdinand Marcos) tried anticipating future ouster by creating plans to ferret out their enemies from within. The worst is Xi who pretends to be strong by bullying us.

The leadership of President Rodrigo Duterte shows adherence to the rule of law even when it was not during his term that the country went to PCA at the Hague for arbitration. President Duterte's concern is to preserve peace in the region and war is definitely not the answer to solve the territorial disputes.

Pres. Duterte is correct, we will not start a fight with China, its the right strategy. We just want to get what is due us especially our fishermen through co-existence and to have freedom to sail and catch fish and other marine life in the SCS-WPS area.

Actually, Xi's bullying is an art of war so as not to show his domestic problems and weaknesses. The situation in China will not be a repeat of Tiananmen Square incident because Xi is fighting so many fronts from within this time. He has to heed Deng Xiao Ping's popular warning that if there will be a Chinese tyrant leader,a bully and aggressor, the people of the world should work together with the Chinese people to overthrow it, a possible truth that could happen anytime soon.

Ooooo

JULY 19, 2016
Anti-Drugs Déjà vu

This three-month reign of perceived police terror left at least 2,274 people dead. The government and police implausibly ascribed the deaths to gangland feuding, insisting that only 42 drug suspects were shot by police officers "most of those in self-defense". In fact, the government openly encouraged the police to carry out extra-judicial killings so that the arbitrary goals of its war on drugs could be met on time.

The Narcotics Control Board provided the indices: 1,765 people arrested as major drug dealers and another 15,244 as minor dealers. More than 280,000 drug pushers and addicts gave themselves up to authorities and were sent for rehabilitation. In all, some 15.5 million pills were confiscated and the street price for the drug doubled or trebled over the course of the three months from February 1 to April 30.

Sounds familiar! In Thailand's 75 provinces, it reported that they had more than fulfilled their quota of reducing the number of drug dealers by 50 percent. In some cases, officials boasted of a 100 percent success rate that is, all drug dealers in their province either dead or detained. Interior Minister Wan Muhammad Nor Matha claimed that 440 local officials and politicians, including two police colonels, had been dismissed because of links to drug trafficking.

The Thai government used a system of bribes and threats to ensure that regional governors and police chiefs carried out the campaign. Three lists were compiled: one by police; the second by local administrative organizations and village heads; and the last by the Narcotics Control Board. Officials who failed to meet their quotas faced dismissal. Those who brought in a major drug dealer "dead or alive" received a bounty of one million baht ($US23,600).

But just who has been arrested or gunned down is unclear, as the allegations against those on the blacklists have not been tested in a court of law. Those whose names appeared had no way of finding out the nature of the accusations against them. Terrified of being framed up or shot dead, thousands opted to hand themselves in and submit to a course of boot-camp style rehabilitation. (Source: Susanne Ilchmann, May 9, 2003)

The above-mentioned scenario looks almost similar to what is happening in our country under the newly installed presidency of Rodrigo Duterte and his war on drugs. With the ever growing number of individuals surrendering to the authorities, from drug users to drug pushers, the current problem now is where to put these people for rehabilitation.

Even before the election day, several people involved in illegal drugs surrendered or face the consequences of being shot to death. The power of President Duterte's words against drug use and its proliferation in the society made them surrender. But for every popular campaign that might involve lives of people and its impact in the community has a corresponding reaction, may it be positive or negative. In our case, and in Thailand under Prime Minister Thaksin, a former chief of police, the human rights advocates are the ones seeking justice for those who were victims of extrajudicial killings and summary executions.

This is one of the reasons for the ouster of Thailand's Prime Minister Thaksin Shinawatra (aside from other accusations like corruption and other government policies), to wit: The Nation (an English-language newspaper in Thailand) reported on November 27, 2007:

"Of 2,500 deaths in the government's war on drugs in 2003, a fact-finding panel has found that more than half was not involved in drug at all. At a brainstorming session, a representative from the Office of Narcotics Control Board (ONCB) disclosed that as many as 1,400 people were killed and labeled as drug suspects despite the fact that they had no link to drugs. ... Senior public prosecutor Kunlapon Ponlawan said it was not difficult to investigate extra-judicial killings carried out by police officers as the trigger-pullers usually confessed." (Wikipedia)

There were reports that Thailand's war on drugs ended up a failure after all until PM Thaksin's ouster in 2006. One factor to be considered seriously was the cross-border trafficking of drugs and the issue on drug lords.

Thailand's War on Drugs victory was temporary. PM Thaksin's campaign has decimated the drug market at the local drug trafficker and street-user level, but it has not reduced cross-border trafficking or attacked the drug trade's higher elements. Additionally, his battle against "Dark Influences" has been ineffective, with few arrests of note. Thailand's King has even tactfully admonished PM Thaksin for his ebullient trumpeting of a victory, when in fact the war is far from over. Burma and Laos are still major contributors to Thailand's drug problem, and most major Thai drug lords remain free. In fact, traffickers have simply changed routes or are storing their product in border areas awaiting a time for safe shipment.

While Thaksin's "war" has had a major impact on Thailand's drug problem, it should be viewed as a relatively successful campaign in a long war, and not as a victorious end to the war itself.(Ibid)

The international community is closely watching the ongoing war on drugs of Duterte's administration and there are global organizations (known for its hands on regime change of some nations) that are critical on its judgment that if you do not kowtow to its policies and so-called international standards, you are headed towards the exit door like what happened to our neighbor" Thailand.

President Duterte has to act fast before his enemies could re-group and destroy him and his loop. Blackmail operation is on. Try to analyze some of the columnists hinting that the president and some of his trusted men have one way or another have links with the top honchos of the underworld.

Many hopes that the president's promise of getting the big fishes is for real. Act fast Mr. President and avoid a deja vu of Thaksin's downfall.

Ooooo

JULY 13, 2016
WPS: Foreign Policy Shift

After the long wait, the United Nation Permanent Court of Arbitration (PCA) released its decision and is still trending on the internet.

And we thought we are done with so much politics after the recent elections and the continuous movement of political butterflies from one party to another, think again.

In the article of Anthony Carlucci, The Politics Behind the Philippines vs. China Court Case, he writes: "The corporate-financier funded and directed policy think tank, the Council on Foreign Relations (CFR) published a paper titled, "Revising U.S. Grand Strategy Toward China," penned by Robert Blackwill – a Bush era administrator and lobbyist who has directly participated in Washington's attempts to maintain hegemony over Asia.

Blackwill's paper states (emphasis added):

"Because the American effort to 'integrate' China into the liberal international order has now generated new threats to U.S. primacy in Asia—and could result in a consequential challenge to American power globally—Washington needs a new grand strategy toward China that centers on balancing the rise of Chinese power rather than continuing to assist its ascendancy.

Indeed, a US policymaker openly admits that the US perceived itself as possessing and seeking to maintain 'primacy in Asia', primacy being defined by Merriam-Webster as, "the state of being most important or strongest."

The United States then, literally an ocean away from Asia, presumes 'primacy' over an entire region of the planet, and is openly seeking to deny the very nations within that region 'primacy' over their own destiny, people and resources.

It is an open, modern proclamation of imperialism.

It is also the true reality that underlines US foreign policy in the South China Sea and explains why an American and British, not only a Philippine legal team has spent years trying to exact a ruling from the UN and other 'international' organizations regarding Beijing.

In this context, it is quite clear why Beijing plans to ignore the ruling."

Indeed, since the very start, a lot of thinking Filipinos wondered why we have an Anglo-American panel of lawyers who handled our case at The Hague because they were worried about the cost (in dollars) of these lawyers and its impact when the ruling was released. But the mere fact we had a leadership of 'slaves' then kowtowing to a perceived master, this foreign-led pool of lawyers went ahead to 'help' us win the court battle. And the irony began when we are fighting for sovereignty over territories while we have given up our sovereignty to be represented by foreigners. Tell me, is that a big B.S. or not?

Can we blame China for not believing in the PCA decision?

In his another article, The Philippines vs. China Case is a US Stunt, Carlucci reminds Asians that the "Philippines vs. China Hague ruling" is meaningless for ASEAN. It is a court case in which a US law firm is representing the Philippines against China, from which the Philippines has absolutely nothing to gain except a growing, senseless, and costly confrontation with China.

The perception is that the US however, gets to use the case to further divide and destabilize the region while giving itself an opportunity to reassert its hegemony in the region.

We are adviced that ASEAN had better not fool themselves into thinking they have anything to gain by playing part in this. This is about dividing and weakening ALL of Asia. The US says so in its own policy papers.

If ASEAN wants to navigate this ruling intelligently, it will dismiss it as a public relations stunt, and continue seeking a bilateral settlement for whatever the problem actually is in the South China Sea with China directly.

We are told by the same paper that if the ASEAN tries opportunistically to use these US-backed stunts against China, they will eventually find themselves the victims of such stunts in the near future.

Asia's future must be determined by Asia – not by Western-controlled 'international institutions" or by the US and its meddling."

Very well said, pundits agree that as Asians we have to confront our problems in the region without the meddling of 'other parties' whose possible interest and intention is to create chaos in the process and balkanize the region into warring sovereign states.

This is the wisdom we saw with our new president Duterte, he will find solutions to the territorial disputes with China through bilateral talks and bilateral projects in the mineral-rich South China Sea/West Philippines Sea and avoid confrontation.

Now that the International Arbitration Court ruled in favor of the Philippine rights in the sea dispute. We also have to remind the leadership of China that they are also a signatory to UNCLOS, the rule of law must prevail. Let us not submerge the West Philippine Sea into chaos but instead let us cooperate to develop the region so that Asians will gain from it.

Let our neighborhood be the ground for mediation between the two superpowers so that peace will be ensured and not be the battleground and prelude to the next world war.

Ooooo

JULY 6, 2016
How The Triad Drug Cartel Controlled the Nation

Finally, drug operations in the Philippines is now truly being addressed. Thanks to the strong will of President Rodrigo Duterte. But how this nationwide operation came about and now already embedded even to the highest and smallest fiber of our society?

The British opium operation in China was exported in Hong Kong and to some parts of Asia including the Philippines. Even in the books of Jose Rizal, he exposed how even our so called Illustrados were used by Chinese businessmen and barter traders to bring in opium to the country in disguise as support to finance their revolution. Even the NPA's in the mountain provinces plant marijuana to support their cause.

The Triad Gang of China was in gambling, prostitution, smuggling, trading opium to producing shabu, money lending and laundering.

A book manuscript of Col. Balbino Diego, former FM's PSC (Presidential Security Command) chief legal, tycoons like Li Ka Shing of Hong Kong, Stanley Ho of Macau and Run Run Shaw of Singapore were part of the Triad.

Under the Marcos regime, a mafia – like code of silence was strictly observed to hide illicit transactions with the Triad using their underworld connections to smuggle including war loots especially gold.

When the US government found out this secret connection of Marcos with the underworld, FM was forced to create his own legitimate Chinese connection by creating his own dummies like Henry Sy, Jose Yao Campos, etc.

To avert his link with the Triad, he discreetly ordered the burning of the floating casino of Stanley Ho to justify the discontinuity of Ho's operation. Diego orchestrated the killing of the chemist of FM's Triad asset, a certain Co. Lim Seng, the chemist of Co from China didn't even understand English nor Tagalog. Lim Seng was told by Co that he will be killed in disguise using dud bullets. FM ordered to shoot Lim Seng via musketry to show to the world that he is against drug proliferation.

FM sent his children abroad to study and avoid friends with bad influence, especially those using downers, marijuana and other prohibited high end drugs. Remember the plane crushed during the time of Marcos where most of the 'friends' of Bongbong Marcos died? An accident in disguise?

When Marcos and family went to China and visited Mao Tze Tung, he secretly invested his war loots of precious metals in China, claiming that it's payback time and admitted to Mao that his real father was a businessman from Amoy, China named Andres Chua, a rice miller in Ilocos Norte.

In the 80's, FM laundered money with the help of an American insurance company with direct connection in Hong Kong and China. Hot monies were poured in the Philippine financial system. The Binondo Central Bank of then Finance Minister Bobby Ongpin managed the underground economy.

In my previous report which I have written a summary and can be read at my blog, I have shown how our government was penetrated by Chinese underworld through some government officials like Marcos, head of G2

(AFP), then Gen. Pedro dela Pena and other military and police officers and big business including media owners.

Now these Chinese front men of our politicians control basically everything including the Church hierarchy disguised themselves as philanthropists.

The Triad gang expanded and metamorphosed in the late 90's and was called the Six Golden Triad and with Bamboo Gang of Taiwan and 14K of Hong Kong included. Meaning from 3 they became an elite member of 18 Chinese mafia boss worldwide.

Triad History

The term 'Triad' was given by the Hong Kong government to Chinese secret societies based on the triangular symbol which once represented such societies. The symbol is the Chinese character 'Hung,' encased in a triangle, representing the union of heaven, earth, and man. So Triads even today are sometimes referred to as the 'Hung Society' or the 'Heaven and Earth Society.'

The commonly accepted myth about triads is that they began as a resistance movement to the Manchu emperors. The Manchu were from a country north of China (Manchuria) and were seen as foreign rulers, who took China's northern capital (Peking now Beijing) by force, and established their dynasty around 1674.

The Chinese Nationalist government was established in Nanking during 1927 and led by a known killer and criminal member of the Shang Hai Green Gang, Chiang Kai Shek.

Triads took over the government of southern China, fought the Communists (later under Mao Tse Tung) for total control, and Western powers used this "Green Gang" organized crime group to suppress any labor unrest and kill-off communists.

When Japan invaded most major China cities in World War II, Triads offered to work for them instead. In Hong Kong, Triads ran criminal enterprises for Japan while Japan united the gangs under an association called the "Hing Ah Kee Kwan" (Asia Flourishing Organization).

The gangsters were used to help police the residents of Hong Kong, and to suppress any anti-Japanese activity. The gangs were paid through a Japan front company named LEE YUEN COMPANY.

Following World War II, the target of the West and the Triads became Communists again, and the Chiang Kai

Shek nationalist government campaigned to increase Triad membership. In Southern China, this campaign was under Nationalist Army Lieutenant General Kot Siu Wong whose headquarters were at: Number 14, Po Wah Road, Canton where the name of the "14 K" Triad is thought to have originated. It was estimated that in 1947, there were 300,000 Triad members in Hong Kong alone.

When the Mao Tse Tung communists were victorious by 1949, these Triad nationalists were dispersed to Hong Kong, Macao, Thailand, San Francisco, Vancouver, and Perth Australia while the remnants of the Chiang Kai Shek KMT (Kuomintang) South China Army was forced into the Burma highlands where they became pivotal to smuggling drugs to the West via Thailand under Khun Sa. The Communists suppressed Triads on the mainland, executing and imprisoning many. Mao's Prime Minister Chou En Lai banned cultivation and use of opium in 1950.

At its most basic level, the hierarchy of triad members matters little except in each individual relationship between two members, each based on ties between the Dai Lo (big brother) and Sai Lo (little brother). The big brothers give work, protection, and advice to the younger brothers who give loyalty, support, and money in exchange. In many cases, this is the only relationship that matters.

But there is a Triad hierarchy. It is not really known to what extent it is still used. Most analysts agree the lower level ranks are still commonly in place, but how many Triad groups use the more complicated higher rankings and to what extent cannot be accurately measured. Along with the names of each rank, Triad ranks also have numbers, all beginning with the number 4, which represents the four oceans said to surround China in ancient times, and therefore signifying the universe as a whole. (Source: China Triad Secret Societies Bank Trillions by Unwanted Publicity Intelligence - Staff Writer, November 2008)

At the end of President Fidel Ramos regime, i wrote an article, "Narco-politics will Control Future Administrations" which was published in several newspapers. Sad to say, they did. Even in the 2010 elections, there were reports that "narco-politics has become a major issue in the Philippine election campaign following the release of a US state department report in which it expressed concern that the illicit drug trade may influence the outcome of the May 10 poll.

The state department's 2010 International Narcotics Control Strategy Report, made public March 1, 2010 said the illegal narcotics trade "continues to pose a significant national threat, especially in view of the coming national elections". According to the Philippine Drug Enforcement Agency (PDEA), the illegal drugs trade in the country totals US$6 billion to $8bn annually and is growing.

"Narco-politics is a serious concern in our country and is growing," said Gilbert Teodoro, a former defense secretary, said he was aware of the claims made in the state department report but added: "the problem does not involve politicians at the national level". "The problem is at the local and provincial levels especially in some parts of Mindanao," he told the Manila Overseas Press Club on March 5.

The former chairman of the Dangerous Drugs Board, Vicente Sotto, who ran for a Senate seat, said some candidates' campaigns had "probably already been infiltrated" by drug lords but were unaware of it. He said the best advice for local politicians is not to accept campaign contributions from unknown sources. The Commission on Elections, which oversees the electoral process, said the reports were "quite alarming" and asked the PDEA to name those candidates who are alleged to be receiving drug money from traffickers for their campaign." (Source: Philippines poll 'hit by drugs trade' by Karl Wilson, March 15, 2010).

There were already reports and possibilities were high even in the 2010 elections of narco-politics or the use of drug money for campaign funds, but what is the difference compared to the Duterte administration now? Our present leadership has enough courage and sincerity to stop this menace – proliferation of illegal drugs and has given names of high-ranking police officials who are reportedly protecting people who are in the drug trade.

The list of President Duterte is long and I am pretty sure that in due time he will name names again. Beware, the change is here and Pres. Duterte is very angry to those who are actually committing treason in the process. This is the right for the nation to support a righteous leader's out of the box agenda.

Ooooo

JUNE 27, 2016
SCS Issue: Can be managed but not resolved?

A UN tribunal ruling could trigger the next round of brinkmanship in the South China Sea as early as next week. But don't expect the ruling to end the dispute, especially since the Chinese have already vowed to ignore an adverse ruling.

"It's…not likely to be resolved this year or by one international ruling, no matter how brilliant the arbitrators are," said Patrick Cronin of the Center for a New American Security. "So it's going to be a long term issue for the next administration." (UN Ruling Won't End South China Sea Dispute: Navy Studies Next Clash by Sydney J. Freedberg, Jr. 6-20-2016)

Anytime soon the much awaited United Nations tribunal's decision will be released and this will come in time of the biennial large-scale multinational power projection/sea control exercise called Rim of the Pacific Exercise (RIMPAC) 2016.

Conducted biennially (every even year) under the leadership of the US Third Fleet, RIMPAC is a multinational, combined sea mobility exercise in which the ROK, US, Australia, Canada, Chile, England, and Japan have participated since 1971. RIMPAC is designed to enhance the tactical capabilities and cooperation of participating nations in various aspects of maritime operations at sea.

The exercise is held with the objective of increasing mutual cooperation and enhancing the combined operations capabilities among the countries around the rim of the Pacific Ocean so that they can ensure the safety of major sea lines of communication (SLOCs) and improve their combined response capabilities in the event of conflict on the sea.

China's debut in the world's largest naval exercise is a "leap of trust" as it teams with the United States and U.S. allies at a time of heightened regional tension over territorial disputes in 2014.

Despite growing tensions between China and United States and its allies over the "militarization" of the

South China Sea, China's navy confirmed last June 2 that it will take part in RIMPAC, one of the world's largest military exercises. China sent five ships to join the Pacific Rim military exercises, that began on June 1 and will last until August 1, near the Hawaiian Islands. China's Defense Ministry said that a fleet of its naval vessels is heading for Hawaii to join US-led multinational naval drills. The ministry said the fleet arrived at waters south of Japan's Daito Islands on Saturday and joined 2 US Navy destroyers there. The 5 Chinese vessels, including a missile destroyer and a frigate, will engage in electronic communication training with the US Navy en route. They are scheduled to arrive in Hawaii on June 29th.

According to official reports, 45 ships, five submarines and 200 aircraft from 27 nations, with 25,000 military personnel, will take part in the event, staging fire, anti-piracy, search and rescue, and, notably, Aegis missile-interception drills. Three Aegis-equipped fleets, from the US, Japan and South Korea, will practice intelligence coordination amid growing concerns of North Korea's nuclear weapons program. This year's exercise includes forces from Australia, Brazil, Brunei, Canada, Chile, Colombia, Denmark, France, Germany, India, Indonesia, Italy, Japan, Malaysia, Mexico, the Netherlands, New Zealand, Norway, China, Peru, the Republic of Korea, the Philippines, Singapore, Thailand, Tonga, the United Kingdom and the United States. Russia took part in RIMPAC in 2012, but canceled its participation in 2014, due to interrupted military cooperation between Moscow and Washington over ongoing territorial disputes in Ukraine. (globalsecurity.org)

There will be live ammunitions during the said exercise and our fear that there might be a miscalculation or a false flag op in the process might lead to an escalation of tension and hell will break loose, a convenient excuse? And who will benefit?

The following are from analysts that will somehow give us ideas on the possible scenario after the release of the UN Tribunal decision.

According to Cronin, "There's some hope after the UNCLOS ruling that we're going to be at least managing the tensions. China could certainly escalate if they desired, but lately, he said, "the Chinese have been looking to ratchet down the tensions even while they've tried to move their influence forward." In other words, don't expect fighting, but don't expect acquiescence to the UN ruling either.

"Patrick Cronin is right: The ruling solves nothing, nor was it meant to," Gregory Poling of the Center for Strategic & International Security. "It will add additional pressure on Beijing, and it will help define the boundaries of any future negotiations — likely years away — but it cannot resolve the disputes."

Far from resolving disputes, agreed fellow CSIS scholar Bonnie Glaser, "the ruling is likely to increase tensions at least in the near term. In a sense it already has, as China has rejected the ruling, and many countries of the world have taken sides, with the US seeking to rally nations in support of international law and a rules based order — i.e. against China's rejection."

"In the short term, we'll probably see China engage in some new escalation to punish Manila and signal that it will not be bound by the ruling," Poling said. For example, said Glaser, "China may establish baselines for its territorial claims in the Spratlys, a precursor to announcing an ADIZ (Air Defense Identification Zone)."

Besides the legal and maritime maneuverings, Poling said, "we will also see the start of the next phase of the battle over competing narratives, this time focused on how many countries Manila and friends can get to voice public support for the ruling as legally binding and demand China complies. The question will be, whether or not they can maintain that pressure from a broad swath of countries over the long term" in the face of Chinese diplomatic and economic pressure.

"The South China Sea territorial disputes are likely to persist for a long time," said Glaser. "The question is whether they can be managed, not resolved." (Source: Sydney J. Freedberg Jr.)

In these exciting times, in the midst of the biggest military exercise, let us all be prepared and hope for something better as we await the UN tribunal ruling. And with the incoming president, with his wisdom, we pray that the SCS dispute can still be managed and war can be avoided.

Ooooo

June 22, 2016
New Opportunities

"Are you with us or are you not with us?"

A question raised by President-elect Rodrigo Duterte to US Ambassador Philip Goldberg in a recent meeting in Davao City. And Amb. Goldberg answered, "Only if you are attacked."

Is this a valid answer coming from a long-time ally? I believe so, as an observer of events, we have written about this on how far the US can extend its helping hand when our country will be needing the Big Brother's help.

Yes, for a time we have doubts on Washington's sincerity in extending its support to us if ever we will encounter a military clash with our neighbors specifically with China on the South China Sea issue. This is because of the close economic ties between US and China and its bilateral meetings on military matters in the Pacific region.

Even though we have several treaties with the US on defense and security, as we know, these treaties are lopsided and we are at the losing end and yet our leaders seem not to bother to correct such wrongs.

Now that the country's incoming president asked that crucial question, it is a good start to check our relationship with Uncle Sam. And during the campaign President Elect Duterte said that we have to change some of our foreign policy and be less dependent with the US.

As the incoming president, and it is a little over a week to take the seat of the highest office of the land, incoming President Duterte has to wait for some of the ongoing developments in the country. One such issue is the upcoming decision that will come from the Permanent Court of Arbitration from The Hague on the territorial dispute on the South China Sea.

As what my friend Prof. Rommel C. Banlaoi wrote in his commentary in RSIS (Rajaratnam School of International Studies) – "The Duterte presidency could open many opportunities for the improvement of Philippines-China political relations. But Duterte has to be cognizant of two major challenges that might affect his administration's achievement of that goal: The first is the result of the international arbitration of the South China Sea dispute between the Philippine government and China. The Permanent Court of Arbitration (PCA) at The Hague is expected to render its decision soon. Should the International Arbitral Tribunal not offer the Philippines a total legal victory on the case, even a partial legal victory can yield some political purposes domestically and internationally."

Duterte has the option of using the result of the arbitration as his main political leverage in resuming bilateral talks with China. But there is a strong likelihood that Duterte will not pursue this option, as China will not want to see him raising the arbitration case in the process of resuming any bilateral discussions on the South China Sea disputes.

As a confidence building measure, it is likely that Duterte will keep mum on the arbitration result and set it aside for the time being while his administration exerts efforts to repair the Philippines' damaged political ties with China. But there is no way for the Duterte administration to withdraw from the arbitration process because of domestic and international considerations.

Domestically, the arbitration case has the approval not only of the Filipino public but also of key national leaders involving past presidents, the senate president, the speaker of the house, justices of the supreme court and concerned department secretaries. Internationally, the international arbitration case has the support of the Philippines' security ally, the United States, and other strategic partners in regional security like Japan, Australia, South Korea, and key members of the European Union and Asean. Especially now that the ASEAN integration is in the offing. The globalists are very optimistic of the Asean economic and geo-political unification. No spoiler state will be tolerated.

But if bilateral talks with China fail to bear fruit that will redound to the benefit of the Filipino people, particularly on Filipino fishermen who are greatly affected by sea disputes, Duterte can use the arbitration decision as a fall back option. Thus, China also needs to exert its own efforts in fixing its broken political relationship with the Philippines as it takes two to tango, so to speak.

The second is the implementation of the Enhance Defence Cooperation Agreement (EDCA) with the US. The Duterte administration is duty bound to implement EDCA considering that the Philippine Supreme Court already declared its constitutionality. Moreover, the Philippines remains as a security ally of the US which views EDCA as a tool to enhance this alliance. While Duterte will not put any obstacle to the EDCA's implementation, his administration will avoid the previous administration's excessive pro-Americanism of embracing Philippine-American alliance at the expense of Philippines-China political ties."

The incoming president has to play his cards well so as not to hurt any feelings from the diplomatic circle but the most important factor is his commitment to the Filipino people above everything else.

For now, we are in a wait and see mode but as far as President elect Duterte's pronouncements on very crucial issues is concern, the Filipinos are satisfied compared to the (almost) past administration.

May God grant him wisdom to lead this country towards greatness and be respected by the rest of the world in the process.

Ooooo